Recovery
Tower

Ronald Simmons

Table of Content

Introduction

For years I asked God to show me how to effectively explain the process called recovery to Ministers, loved ones, people who work in the field of recovery, and especially to people who are seeking recovery for themselves.

In 1997 I was asked to share with a group of Ministers in San Diego and explain the 12 Steps and the Process of Recovery. After leaving that meeting it was obvious they still had no clue what Recovery was. On the train ride back to Los Angeles I pleaded with God to help me paint the picture of Recovery because it was no use in continuing if the most powerful organization in our community "The Church" could not get behind this awesome move of God. On that train ride home God gave me the *Recovery Tower*.

This journey begins in a building that has twelve floors, which I refer to as *Recovery Tower*. Each floor in this building represents one of the twelve spiritual ways to recovery. Here, at *Recovery Tower*, many people are given an opportunity to get their lives together as they are introduced to recovery. Some accept the challenge and progress through this building, picking up tools along the way that will help them to remain in recovery. Others decide, though their actions that the journey is too difficult, and this journey is too challenging for them; so they start over or leave the building altogether.

Those who attempt to complete this journey travel from floor to floor learn more about God and the process as they go.

Crashing and Burning

There's No Bottom Like This Bottom

My name is Frank G., and I am a computer programmer by profession. I come from a middle class family that gave me everything I needed, but not necessarily everything I wanted. I wish I could tell you that I came from a broken home, but I didn't. My mother and father worked to give us everything. I was taught right from wrong at a very young age and it was in my high school days that I chose the wrong path because it seemed like more fun. All of my life, I saw alcoholics and addicts on the street, but I never thought I would become one.

I can remember taking my first drink and smoking my first joint and no way did I think I'd become addicted to either one. Who knew that one beer would turn into a daily six pack or a craving for hard liquor? How quickly my life changed when one joint became too many and alcohol had me staggering down the street. I wish I could tell you when I crossed the line into addiction but I can't.

One day I was having fun and then one day it was killing me. When I had it I used it and when I didn't have it I spent most of my time thinking about how I could get it. What started out to be something I thought I could control was now playing me like a puppet on a string. It had gotten so bad that I wanted to die, but it seem like the devil got pleasure in watching me struggle.

For the last four years, I have been on a downward spiral. Every time I thought I hit bottom, a trap door opened and I fell deeper into this bottomless pit called addiction. Everything I touched seemed to blow up in my face. I lost a good job because I was too high to show up. I lost the best girlfriend I ever had because the drugs, now, came first and she became second. I got kicked out of my apartment and my family members were tired of bailing me out of trouble and hearing my excuses. To tell you the truth, I was tired of coming up with new ones.

In the beginning, I tried to blame it on bad luck, bad choices, or the jealousy of everyone around me. After a while, it was easy to see that using drugs and alcohol caused all my problems.

Today, my family has cut all ties with me. I believe they all got together and came up with a plan on how they were going to deal with me. Every time I showed up at any of my family members' doors, they made certain they gave me no money; however, if I was hungry, they fed me (Conspiracy I tell you).

None of my relatives would let me in their homes unattended - only to shower or eat. They started going to these "Tough Love – co-dependent meetings" where they learned how to deal with someone with a problem like mine. I hated them for that, it seem like everybody was turning against me, even my mother! She told me they had all had "Turned me over to God." At that time, I thought my family's tough-love tactics were cold and heartless, but this approach turned out to be the best thing that ever happened to me!

One day after finding myself homeless and hungry, I ran into an old friend named Daniel. Daniel and I used to drink and get high together, but one day, Daniel just disappeared. We all thought he ended up in jail or maybe died on the street somewhere. However, that was far from the case.

Daniel was alive and well and he looked like a million dollars. He had put on weight, his skin color was clear, and he had money in his pocket. But more important, he had a look about himself that was hard to explain.

He asked me was I tired of living the way I had been living. I tried to act like I had no idea what he was talking about, but I had no energy to keep up the façade anymore. I told him that I was not only tired, but the thrill of getting high was gone. I couldn't tell him why I still did it.

The fun of getting high had disappeared a long time ago. Feeling helpless and hopeless the last thing I wanted to do was cry in front of another man, but a tear began to trickle down my cheek. I had no idea what I was going to do. Life wasn't worth living.

He then reached in his pocket and handed me a card with an address to a place where I could find relief and get some help. This place is called *Recovery Tower*, he said located on the east side of town. He told me that *Recovery Tower* is where he found freedom, a place where addicts and alcoholics find help.

Any other time I would have gotten upset with someone calling me an addict or alcoholic but there was no fight left in me. What Daniel had I wanted, and if Daniel could get it I knew I had a chance to get it because he smoked and drank just as much as me. Daniel called it "Freedom" and this is what I saw in Daniel's eyes. If this place could help Daniel, it was no doubt in my mind it could help me.

He was a hope to die drunk that people laughed at and talked about. He was the kind of guy that no one ever thought would amount to anything. Now, this person who was voted most likely to go to prison or lose his mind was standing before me drug free and now I'm the one people are laughing at.

Life starts in the Basement

Got to start somewhere!

A 12 Step Program Anywhere In the World

Daniel told me that, at this place called *Recovery Tower*, recovery begins in the basement.

People that are trying to save their lives have one thing in common. They have all hit a bottom. Evidently hitting a bottom is the result of one's countless attempts to stop drinking and using only to find themselves drinking and using again.

I don't know how many times I secretly tried to stop, always devising plans to curb my drinking and using or to stop completely. With each failing attempt I slowly ran out of new ways of quitting. The energy to stop was draining and exhausting and it took everything in me to try again. Drinking, using, and the attempts to quit was like riding an out of control merry-go-round where nothing was merry any more.

Daniel went on to say that once a person hits a bottom, that person's life is now unmanageable, whether it is financial, socially, mentally or health-wise. This individual's life is a complete mess. For some, a bottom may be defined as losing their job which, consequently, will force them to seek help. Some may have to lose family members, material things and friends before they are willing to get help. Others will go to jail or experience near-death situations and still others have to experience all of the above in order for them to realize that they are out of control and are in need of some type of help.

I asked Daniel to lend me some money because I could not remember the last time I had eaten and, then, I would check myself into *Recovery Tower*. Daniel bought me a burger and told me that was the best that he could do for me. He then shook my hand and while holding my hand said a quick prayer for me and he turned and left.

This place called *Recovery Tower* was across town, and I had no money to get there. My feet were hurting and it seemed like I had been walking for days, wandering from one dope house to another. I was determined to get to this place called *Recovery Tower*. At that moment, a bus was approaching. The bus pulled up right in front of me.

The door opened and I asked the bus driver if he was he going to the east side. I told him I had no money, but I was headed to a place called *Recovery Tower*. He smiled and told me he was going right by there and told me to hop on. I found a seat right behind the driver and began to think that luck was finally on my side. First, I ran into an old friend who told me about this place called *Recovery Tower* and, now, a bus driver gives me a free ride there.

Before I could say anything, he told me he was a graduate of *Recovery Tower* and that we have to take care of our own. He went on to say that in order for him to keep this freedom called recovery, he had to give it away. I sat behind him as we drove towards the east side. He continued to share his testimony and it was a lot like mine. I was amazed that he didn't care who heard him as he shared in great detail how he had hit his bottom, all while stopping at each bus stop to pick up and drop off passengers.

As the bus pulled up in front of a brick building on the east side, the doors opened and the bus driver turned and looked at me and said, "This is it, buddy." Before I stepped off of the bus, I turned to thank him and he said, "Give yourself a break, and don't leave five minutes before the miracle happens. He closed the door and pulled off.

The building looked about twelve stories high, and a large arrow pointing towards a set of stairs that led down the outside of the building. After going down about two flights of stairs there was a half-cracked door at the bottom of the stairs. Over the door was a sign that said "Basement"

I slowly pushed the door open that entered inside this larger room. No one was there to greet me, there was no official sign in and I began to think am I in the right place? As I looked around the room, I figured this must be the place because most of the people here look just like me. They looked as if they had been in a 12-round bout with the heavy weight champion of the world. Another sign on the wall read "The Basement".

There were several tables in this basement with flyers and brochures stacked neatly on them. Also on each table were a large coffee pot and donuts. This looks like a good place to get started. While waiting in a small line to get my coffee, a guy standing in front of me turned around and introduced himself as John. He seemed very comfortable as if he had been here for a while. He told me he had been in this basement for three days now and seem to know a lot about recovery and this building. He also told me he had been in this building before and that any day now he was going to try recovery again. I had no idea what he was talking about but I poured myself some coffee, grabbed a donut, a couple of flyers and a brochure, and then found a seat. I looked up and John was right behind me, so I moved over so he could sit next to me.

John told me that he was married and had a baby on the way; he also worked at the post office as a mail carrier. His wife and kid were staying with parents while he got his life together here at *Recovery Tower*. He told me his drug of choice was crack cocaine and he had been smoking it for years. As we both drank our coffee I began to look over the brochure I picked up from the table.

One flyer was titled, "Its' No Accident That You Are Here". The flyer discussed how God is directing your footsteps and guiding you to this place to get your life together. I chuckled as I thought about my friend Daniel who told me about this place and, then, the bus driver who gave me a ride. I didn't know too much about God, but something happened that was out of my control, which led me here. The brochure was titled, "Surrender to Win". At first, that made no sense. Once I opened the brochure this is what I read!

Stop fighting, this battle it is bigger than you. Each strategic plan to stop drinking and using continues to fail. Rarely does anyone win this battle devising their own plan. Once you've become aware that alcohol and drugs are a problem in your life it's time to seek help.

What we suggest makes no sense. It's not logical and defies everything you were taught while growing up. Surrender To Win?

To many individuals, Surrender to Win is hard to do and to others, even harder to understand. How can anyone Surrender and Win at the same time? For those that struggle with this concept, think back to every dangerous or devastating situation that you've ever been in. If you're reading this brochure a power greater than yourself brought you out. God fixed, moved, or rescued you without your help! So now you may ask what do you do?

How do you get started? It's simple, like in the movies when they catch the bad guy. The first thing you do is throw your hands up in submission. We throw our hands up in surrender to God! We throw our hands up in praise to God, giving Him all our problems.

Surrendering to Win allows God to fix this battle against drug and alcohol addiction. But this time you'll be involved, because you're being taught to "Let Go and Let God". In This battle you will watch God work, and in doing so we give Him all the Glory! Your biggest battle is getting out of the way! God doesn't need your help!

A recorded message began to play over the intercom that said, "Welcome to *Recovery Tower*. If you are willing, your new life can start today!" I thought to myself, "Why wouldn't people be willing? I am so tired of living the way I have been living." The voice over the intercom continued to say, "Many people begin this new life, here, in the basement and their life will be forever changed. But for many, due to a lack of effort and a lack of trust or wanting to do their own thing, some will unfortunately return to the basement over and over again. Then, there are those that never give this new life a chance. They stay in and around the basement forever, surrendering to a hopeless life style.

They adapt to the addicted environment even though the lifestyle is killing them emotionally, mentally, physically, and is affecting them spiritually.

Furthermore, the top priority for everyone on the bottom is to fill the void inside that is crying out for more drugs or alcohol. What you will find out is that only the Spirit of God can fill that void.

Finally, a person walked by with a *Recovery Tower* nametag on her white hospital jacket that read Aletris. I asked Aletris what our next step is. She said, "At some point, each person here in the basement is given a chance to leave the basement. People in recovery call it a "moment of clarity". An "ah ha or I got it" moment. Unfortunately, for most of us it is only a moment. It's a short period of time that will allow you the opportunity to escape or get help.

In the real world "a moment of clarity" may be someone sharing God's goodness with them and that person surrenders all to God. Or it may be a loved one pleading with them to get some help and that person finds assistance. At that moment, the mind considers getting help and in that short window of opportunity the addict and/or alcoholic must take advantage of the help that is before them. It is at this moment that God gives us an opportunity to surrender to freedom. If you do not take advantage of this moment of clarity, fear, or the obsession to drink or use, will overpower that moment and the window of opportunity will close.

Some of you are in that moment right now, so do not blow it, and please take advantage of it." I looked around and a few other people had assembled around us to listen to what Aletris had to say. I didn't know how everyone else was feeling, but every word that came out of Aletris's mouth made sense to me. My moment of clarity was running into Daniel, and the bus driver giving me a ride to this place! Aletris continued to say, "It's like throwing a lifeline out to someone who is drowning. There is nothing you can do if the drowning person does not reach out and grab the line."

Fear is one of the main reasons those facing addiction oftentimes do not grab hold of the lifeline. Fear of change, fear of the unknown, and the fear of being responsible, can keep someone from seeking help. Many recovering people seek help not knowing the amount of work and dedication that is involved in order to stay free one day at a time - forever.

Recognizing the abnormal behavior in their own lives and taking the necessary steps to change these behaviors may seem like an impossible task, but those of you who are truly tired of living in the gutter surrender to this process called recovery. Those that learn to trust in God and take the suggestions of others who have gone before them (because God works through people), learn to live free, face their fears, and conquer those triggers that make them stumble at every turn.

The fear of success causes many to sabotage some of the doors that are open to you. You consciously or unconsciously undermine opportunities that come your way. Not showing up for work, or purposely coming in late to work or not getting along with other employees. These are just a few ways we slowly destroy God given opportunities. The individuals who fear success know that success brings responsibility and responsibility brings accountability. From this position or vantage point, just the thought of others relying on you is overwhelming.

Personal relationships suffer and are damaged as well. Committing to someone with the fear of one day taking a drink or using drugs seems pointless, so many never give their all in relationships. You keep your loved ones at arm's length, but simultaneously disclose enough to run to them when you need help.

You rebel against everyone who comes to your aid, blaming everyone for your failures, hoping to keep attention on others and away from, ignoring the crux of the real problem – the individual who has the problem. Many of you have dug a hole so deep that you do not think it is possible to climb out.

Instead of looking to God to open up doors in your life, you continue looking at the power within yourselves, always ready to come up with another plan to get out of the dilemma without help from anyone. Many of you have to realize that it was your own thinking that got you into the hell you are living in today. But then some of you find it hard to surrender to God because you do not know what to expect and your need to control will not let you surrender. By this time, the crowd grew thicker, and everyone was tuned in on every word to figure out what their next steps would be.

Then there are those who had a relationship with God and now guilt will not let you return to Him. You find it hard to believe that God could love and care for you after feeling like you have turned your back on God. You are ignorant to the fact that addiction is a sickness, so you spend most of your attempts at freedom believing you are bad and undeserving people trying to be good, instead of sick people trying to get well. As a result, you return to what you know best: drinking and using and the destructive lifestyle that accompanies it.

Many of you have been in and out of so many drug and alcohol programs that the thought of going into another program seems like a waste of time. Life begins to look like an unbeatable monster and surrendering to another program for a better life seems pointless. So what is the use?

As a result, you return to your old lifestyles, trying to make the best of living with your addiction. With no hope of things getting any better, you do your best to adapt to the lifestyle that is killing you in almost every way. You try to convince yourself, family, and friends that this lifestyle is not that bad and that you are not hurting anyone but yourself. Then you disappear for days, months, or even years at a time, secretly trying to put some stability back into your life.

You have this idea that you will show up at the next family reunion drug-free and in your right mind. Pipe dreams that never come to pass and continue to pile up until the weight of your drinking and using is too much and now everyone knows.

I didn't know about everybody else but Aletris was stepping all over my toes. One thing that stood out was "I am not a bad person trying to be good, but a sick person trying to get well".

She went on to say hitting a bottom in many cases ends up being a blessing in disguise for many addicts and alcoholics that are too smart to listen to those around them. The bottom for them is too much to bear. The merry-go-round is no longer merry and like the prodigal son, who "came to himself", they too have a "moment of clarity" in which the addict/alcoholic remembers a better life and is willing to do whatever it takes to return to that better lifestyle.

However, to achieve this better lifestyle, the first step must be taken from the bottom, one step at a time toward the top floor. Learning how to be obedient to the instructions that are presented before you will be your life-long quest.

Once you totally surrender to the process of recovery, you must go in with your white flag raised high, surrendering to whatever it takes to gain freedom. You must be willing to take suggestions from people that have been down this road before you, and are now living victoriously.

Those that surrender to the process of recovery stay free from drinking and using one day at a time. Learning how to apply this program to our lives will take the rest of our lives.

There was now at approximately 40 people tuned in to Aletris' every word. I leaned over to John and asked him does he expect us to remember all of this and when are we going to get started? Before John could answer, Aletris told everyone who was ready to take the next step to follow her. I, along with others, jumped up and followed right behind her. She walked up to seven elevators that opened automatically. Above the elevator, a sign read "Moment of Clarity". Most of us jumped on the elevator, before the doors closed. I noticed John was standing on the other side. I yelled at him and tried to stop the doors from closing, but John did not make an attempt to get on. He looked right at me and put his head down as if he didn't want the help that was being offered; he was not ready to move on and receive this help.

As the doors closed, all I could think was, "Why"? "Why didn't John come with us?" He seems like such a nice guy and what about his wife, and baby, and his job? As I stood there stunned, I wondered what would make a person turn his back on all of that. Certainly, he had more to lose than me as I had nothing.

On the inside of the elevator door a sign read "To make it to the top, you must trust and have faith in

God". At that moment, some of the people began to grumble and complain. In the elevator, people were whispering questions like, "How do you trust in God?" "Who is God?" "What is trust?" "What is faith?"

The elevator slowly began to move up towards the first floor when a voice came over the intercom. "Do you believe that this elevator will take you to the floor that you desire without any hurt, harm, or danger? If so, you are putting your faith and trust into something that you know nothing about. Nonetheless, you entered the elevator not giving it another thought. I thought to myself, "That's right." I also noticed that a sense of peace fell on everyone. Once again, the voice said, "Be still and know that He is God." God has been taking care of you when you could not care for yourself".

It was at this time that I started thinking about the pulleys and the motors that allowed this elevator to rise and fall. I thought about the cables that kept this big steel box from falling down into the basement. For some strange reason, I just believed it would take me safely to my destination. I asked myself, "Is this what faith is all about?"

Slowly the elevator came to a complete stop. I had a feeling that this experience was going to be different from anything that I had ever experienced. Once the doors opened, I stepped off onto the first floor with everyone else.

Throw Up The White Flag
Give Yourself A Break!

First Floor

A sign on the wall directly in front of us read "Follow the arrows to the room called CHANGE." On the sign was a large red arrow directing us down a hallway that was painted white and on these walls was more arrows that led us up to a door that entered into the room. On the top of the door a sign read "CHANGE".

As we walked in, we saw chairs lined up in rows with our names printed on each chair, and in front of the chairs was the podium. The room had two doors: one at the front of the room where we entered and the other in the back of the room. Near the back of the room, I noticed a long table with white tee shirts folded neatly on the top. I found my name on a chair near the center of the room. After each of us found our chairs and was seated, a man wearing all white came into the room and stood behind the podium.

He introduced himself as Todd. Todd was a stocky African American with a permanent smile on his face. Todd said "Before I came to *Recovery Tower* I was a hopeless individual. If you want to make it through this process you have to be open to change, you have to learn how to trust in others and take suggestions". As a direct result of my willingness to change, I am now a new person. I am here to tell you that changing will be your biggest obstacle because we, as recovering people, feared the unknown". What he was saying did not make much sense to me; however, one thing Todd said that seem to make sense was, "When there is no change, there is no change." Wow! I thought, so simple, but so profoundly powerful." If I do not change, I will stay the same. I CAN'T LET THAT HAPPEN! I also thought about John in the basement. Maybe that was it. John was not ready to change.

Deep down within, I desired change and, even more importantly, I knew I needed to change. How to make the change manifest itself was the mystery. Todd said "next I am going to give each of you the opportunity to express yourself. We want to know who you are and why you are here. This will be your first step at practicing honesty. You can't be honest with others until you get honest with yourself. This will be your first big step in your quest for freedom. Without honesty, there is no beginning. Addicts and Alcoholics are liars, this is what we've become, this is what we do!

Pressing through the fear of what others think is one thing that you will have to learn how to get past in these rooms called "CHANGE". Remember you are all in the same boat, starting this process called recovery. Why not drop the heavy baggage, called lies and deceit and lighten your load? You who choose not to be honest carry an unnecessary load on your shoulders and that load will get heavier and heavier every day. In your quest to be free from drugs and or alcohol you one day will be able to answer this question "who is the real you"? Trust me there is not one of you who begins recovery that can answer this question. No you are not a doctor, no you are not a construction worker, and no you're not a secretary, that is what you do. Recovery will help you answer that question.

With a big smile, he asked who would like to go first and come to the podium and share. Of course, no one moved. With a big smile he began to pick people out of the group to come up to the podium and share a little about themselves and why they surrendered to recovery at this time. "Wait a minute," I thought, "I'm no speaker" and fear suddenly consumed my body. I was sitting about three rows from the front of the room. Slowly, I began to sink down in my seat, trying my best to hide behind the person in front of me, but he was sliding down in his seat, too.

As I began to listen to some of the stories, I felt compassion for those who shared; I felt the pain of what drinking and using put them through. As he randomly picked people out of the crowd, he picked a woman named Janet, who was a single parent. For years, Janet was involved in an abusive relationship and stayed with this man for 3 years. This led her to abusing alcohol just so she could make it through the day. Janet's three-year-old daughter was staying with her grandmother while Janet tried to get herself together. As the tears began to build up in her eyes, silence filled the room. From the back of the room someone said "It's okay" and Janet returned to her seat.

I thought to myself "Now, that was deep." I would probably drink too if I had to live like that.

As Todd continued picking people out of the audience one by one they shared their stories, but there was a person whose sharing really caught my attention. He introduced himself as "Shorty the crack head". Some people in the room chuckled. Shorty said "I've been through this building before, but left before reaching the top.

The first time I came here to *Recovery Tower* I really wasn't serious; it was my family that made me come here! To get them to stop nagging me I agreed to come". So the first time I couldn't hear anything because I wasn't doing it for me but for my family. The whole time I was here I resented my family and at every turn I looked for a reason to leave. I never got honest with anybody. I never took anything they told me seriously.

Truthfully I really didn't think my problem was that bad. I thought I could go through the motions and learn how to smoke socially and of course I wasn't as bad as you guys, you were real addicts and alcoholics. After butting heads with everyone in authority that was trying to save my life I found a reason to leave early. I returned to drinking and using, except this time it was worse than ever before.

As he spoke, everyone sat up in their seats, glued to every word. He told us that out of all the things he did: the drinking, the using, disappointing his family and friends, the hardest thing to do was to start recovery all over again. He called this process "bouncing back", and he did not know if he had another "bounce back" left.

"Each time I tried to come back to *Recovery Tower*, it got harder and harder and my bottom got deeper and deeper," he said, "and I am afraid that if I don't make it this time I will die out there! Recovery is the last house on the block for me. This time, I'm here for myself."

If I was a betting man I'd bet he was going to make it. The conviction in his voice captured the whole room and it was silent as he returned to his seat.

I could not avoid Todd any longer, and he pointed towards me. As I made my way to the front of the room, my heart was beating a thousand times a minute. When I turned towards my peers to share, I had a hard time looking up and I felt like the biggest loser in the room. Now, I was about to share how my life became such a mess. I was certainly swimming in uncharted waters.

Quickly, I introduced myself and told the group that I have been drinking and using for 13 years and I admitted that I was tired of living the way I had been living. I was tired of being a bum, tired of living on the streets, tired of being separated from my family and my family not trusting me. To be honest, I was just tired of being tired! I sat down because that was as honest as I could get.

After everyone had finished, Todd returned to the podium and told us to go around the room and meet our peers. Once again, I thought to myself "another new experience." Where I come from, you do not go out and introduce yourself to anyone because no one cares.

Sitting next to me was a woman named Carmen. She was a doctor. Carmen was about to lose her license, her livelihood, and her family because of her drinking. To hear her speak, she had dedicated her whole life to school, her practice, and her family; now, she was about to lose it all behind the bottle. The details of her whole life had been planned even down to how many children she was going to have, what school she would attend, and even what neighborhood she would live in. However, there was one thing about her plan she never considered and that was becoming an alcoholic.

She sounded very determined to make it in this building called *Recovery Tower* and as she put it, "get her life back". When she made that comment, I wondered if I wanted my life back. In the state I was in, at that moment, I could not think of anything good about my life. And what would I be going back to?

After we talked for a while, someone tapped me on the shoulder. When I turned around, a hand reached out to shake mine. A big guy with a balding head introduced himself as Ronnie. Earlier Ronnie shared he was a sales man and he dibble-dabbled in stocks and bonds. He told me he really enjoyed what I shared when I went to the podium and that he found it to be very inspiring. (I thought this was strange because all I was trying to do was say enough and sit down.)

He told me he had a wife and four kids and that his marriage was on the rocks. He was also looking at two years in prison for possession and selling illegal drugs. The judge was giving him one more chance to straighten his life out. Ronnie and I shook hands. I began to make my way over to Shorty, the man who had been through this building before. As I got near him, I saw others who were really inspired by what he shared at the podium surrounding him. I decided to return to my seat and hoped I get a chance to talk to him later.

Todd told us to go to the back of the room where there were t-shirts folded neatly on the white table near the rear doorway. I noticed that there was a sign above the table that had instructions that read "Put on these t-shirts before moving on." After we put them on, we realized that the writing on the shirt read, "God will never leave you, nor forsake you."Wow! What a comforting thought, but is it true?

As we walked out of the room called "Change", wearing our T-shirts, we entered into a large hallway with many doors. In this hallway, Todd said "behind each door, you will be faced with a task or an obstacle that would help you to open your eyes. This is not a race, so take your time. The most important thing to remember is to be completely honest and you will begin to understand this process called recovery. Todd then left us and it looks like we would be facing our fist challenge.

The first room we walked into had a sign on the door that read "Powerlessness." This room had more doors; each one labeled with each of our names over the top. I walked over to the door that had my name on it; I noticed a doorbell and a sign that read, "Push". When I pushed the button, a recording began to play. "The faster you accept that there is a power greater than you, the easier this process becomes.

I opened the door, walked in and found myself standing in a room with a big picture window. Through this window, I could see three of my favorite automobiles: the Targa Porsche, a Lamborghini, and a Corvette. Whoever put this room together knew me very well. I looked around the room and saw a large vacuum cleaner. A sign posted next to the vacuum cleaner read, "This vacuum is one of the most powerful vacuum cleaners in the world." As I looked around the room, only half of the room was covered with carpet and the other half was hardwood floor. Over the loud speaker, a voice said, "You have fifteen seconds to vacuum the carpet in this room. If you can clean the carpet in fifteen seconds, you can pick one of these cars for yourself.

On your mark, get set, Go!" "No problem," I thought. I ran to the vacuum cleaner and carried it over to the carpeted side of the room. In the background, I could hear the seconds being counted down. "14...13...12..." I pulled the power cord out of the outlet and began to look for another power outlet near the carpeted side. The only outlet in the room was on the uncarpeted side. The countdown continued, "12...11...10..." I stretched the cord, but it would not reach the outlet and the carpet at the same time. "9...8...7..." I looked at the vacuum cleaner, then the outlet. I couldn't do anything. "6...5...4...3...2...1..." The whole room went black. Everything disappeared. Frustrated I walked out of the room thinking to myself, "What a cruel trick. What was I supposed to learn from that exercise?"

Before I could think about it anymore, one of the instructors came to my aid. He told me his name was Anderson. Anderson looked like a bookworm with a beard and thick mustache and he wore black wire-rimmed glasses. Anderson had a big smile on his face. "What's wrong" he said? I told him someone played a cruel trick on me; Anderson then asked "what did you learned from it". I thought about it and, for the life of me, I could not come up with an answer. He, then, asked a question: "What kind of vacuum was in the room?" I told him that there was a sign in the room that said it was the most powerful vacuum cleaner in the world, but what difference did that make when I couldn't connect to the power.

He smiled and said, "So, it's just like life. It makes no difference how powerful you think you are, or how tough you think you are. If you don't plug into the power source, you will never have any power. Until you connect to the main power source that gives life (God), it will never make any difference. You'll always run on your own will, and you see where that has gotten you. Forget about the power you think you have, or the power people say you have, you must accept the fact that you are powerless.

If you had power, you would have quit drinking and using a long time ago! The only power that you will ever have is the power that God allows you to have. You failed in life, because you never plugged into the power of God. God, who is willing to give you power, is waiting for you to plug into Him. His power keeps the sun and the moon from crashing into the earth, which would totally destroy it and anyone or anything living on it. The same power that keeps the ocean from flooding the beach and consuming everything and anything in its path, this is the power you need to plug into.

Anderson then led me to a room containing a couch that sat in the middle of the floor. He instructed me to have a seat and he told me that someone would come and get me in a few minutes. As I sat down, I noticed a sign on the wall that read: "Hold on tight" and another sign that read, "Don't leave, 5 minutes before the miracle."

After a few minutes of quiet, a man's voice came over the intercom and greeted me. He began by telling me about my early life. He knew my birth date, where I was born, and how many sisters and brothers I had. He also knew the schools I attended from elementary school through college. Then, he started telling me about my childhood and the mischievous things I used to get into when I was a kid. Things that I had not remembered or thought about in years, he knew down to the smallest detail.

He talked about some of the practical jokes I would play on people and about my being the class clown in school. Then it turned negative. I was shocked when he said that I was destined to be a liar, a cheat, and a two-bit criminal, and spend most of my life behind prison bars.

After that, he really got ugly. I could not believe what I was hearing. He said, "You are a dope addict, and you will never be anything but an addict. Your daddy was nothing, so you will never be anything. You're stupid, you're black in a world that hates you, and you were born to be a failure." The same things he said, I remembered hearing when I was a kid. Those words hurt way back then and they still hurt now. The verbal abuse would not end. He continued calling me a liar, a cheat, and said that I could not be trusted. Ten minutes of this madness was nine minutes too long.

Just before I was ready to walk out of the room, Anderson came to my rescue, right in the nick-of-time. He then said, Welcome to the room called

"Powerlessness" Learning to be powerless is one of the most powerful everyday tools used in recovery. Here you will learn that you are powerless over what other people think, write, or say about you." What happened here in this room was out of your control, and without a workable recovery tool to face what you heard, your anger could lead you to drinking or using or even worse.

All of a sudden, I noticed another sign appeared on the wall "There is power in being powerless." I turned to Anderson and said "That makes no sense! How can power and powerless even be used in the same sentence Anderson smile and said it was hard for me to understand in the beginning, but if you think about it, it makes perfect since. It takes a lot of strength not to get upset, to manage your anger. This is why you have to tap into a power greater than yourself to be at peace in the mists of a storm.

People, places and things have a right to be whom and what they are. Trying to control these things will divert you from your primary purpose, which is STAYING CLEAN AND SOBER, and becoming the person God called for you to be.

Anderson then led me out of this mental torture chamber back into the room called "CHANGE". Some of my peers in this crazy building had already made it back to the room. It was good to see some familiar faces. They all looked as dumbfounded as I felt. Having power, being powerless, having no power of our own, yet accepting God's power, which simultaneously gives you power; however, you have to plug into THAT power that was a bit much!

Anderson approached the podium and asked if anyone wanted to share. Carmen, the doctor, quickly got up and stormed to the podium and said, "I am having a problem with all of this, "I am a doctor with my own practice. I have twelve employees and I make life and death decisions every day, and you are telling me I have no power, that's hogwash!" It was plain to see that she disagreed with this powerless concept. With fire in her eyes, she stormed back to her seat.

Anderson returned to the podium and acknowledged Shorty as he raised his hand. I really wanted to hear Shorty's take on this whole thing. Shorty said "This is where I had my problem the first time I came into this building," the idea of giving up all power to receive power was a hard pill to swallow, especially if you have been in charge of your life all your life. After this last relapse, I can clearly see how weak I really am. Today, I can see I have no other choice. I can no longer be the pilot of my own life. If I am going to make it, I have to turn my will and my life over to God".

After a few more people shared their experience in the powerless room and about this newfound concept called powerlessness. Anderson returned to the podium and began to make some sense out of this concept called powerlessness. As he talked, he looked right at Carmen and said, "It doesn't matter how strong or powerful or how much education you have or had, you are in this building because you didn't have enough power to quit drinking."

I looked over at Carmen and I could see she was still upset and I wondered if she heard anything Anderson said. "If we had power, we wouldn't be here,

Anderson uttered, we would be considered controlled drinkers, or sociable users. You would have the power to take one drink or hit and put it down. Once you walk through the doors of rooms like this, sociable drinking and using are forever gone."

Anderson, then, said something that blew me away, and I'm sure it shook others in the room as well. He said, "You were doing your best thinking, operating your best plan for your life, and you ended up an alcoholic and or a dope addict. "Wow," I thought and silence, once again, consumed the room.

He then said "God allows every man and woman to have individual wills and God will not interfere with the will of man. God loves you so much that he will let you do your own thing, follow your own dreams. For some of us He knows how to push us in the direction he wants us to go. All the while, God is hoping that one day you will surrender to his will.

I began to think how I had gotten to this point in my life. It was easy to see that I was the "black sheep" in the family because of the choices that I made. I could not blame it on anyone else but myself. I was the one who ditched school. I was the one who hung out with the wrong crowd. I was the one that experimented with drugs and alcohol and ended up drinking and smoking everything in sight.

When I began to think about how many times I almost lost my life while in the streets or how close I came to being lock up in jail for years, there had to be a power greater than me that allowed me to still be alive today. For sure my best thinking got me here. All of this can't be luck!

Turning my will and life over to God did not seem so farfetched, but too much was happening, I just got here. I've been making my own decisions for so long, but at this point, I was surely ready to give this "powerless concept" a shot. I thought about the giant vacuum cleaner. Without power, it was nothing but a big machine taking up space. Is that what I had become, someone that was just taking up space? Humm, that was a good question.

Then Anderson ended by saying, "So it doesn't make any difference how big you are, or, how smart you think you are, or how much money you have or don't have. The disease we are fighting is bigger than we are, but, more importantly, the battle we are fighting is a spiritual battle, which can only be defeated with spiritual weapons. Within ourselves, we will never have enough power to defeat this problem. If you could, you would have fixed yourself a long time ago. Most of you are a hop, skip, and a jump away from going crazy trying to figure out how to return to a normal life. Sooner or later, you will have to surrender to a power that is greater than you, or you will continue to fight a losing battle."

Anderson was so right. I have been trying to figure out how to quit using for years. I've tried every trick in the book, but nothing has worked. It became clear to me that a power greater than myself was needed to remain free from my addiction. A power greater than myself was required to right the wrongs that I caused in my own life, a power greater than this demon called addiction.

Another thing hit me; by practicing powerlessness, I am admitting to myself that God has all power. This will be my first step in turning all power over to him. It sounded easy, yet for people like me who ran everything and controlled my own life, old habits are hard to break. Implementing this concept into my life would certainly be an uphill battle. Janet who was sitting next to me leaned over and whispered, "Does this mean we have to turn every waking moment over to God? Isn't God busy? Can't I guide and direct some parts of my life? If not, I've got a long way to go." We both laughed and turn our attention to Anderson who was still sharing.

Anderson asked all of us to bow our heads while he prayed God's blessings upon us and he dismissed us from this room called CHANGE. He then directed everyone down the hall to another door that we all lined up to walk through.

Still on the first floor we walked up to a room that was titled, WILLINGNESS. The signs on the walls of this room read, - By Any Means Necessary - God Will Never Leave You Or Forsake You. Another sign read, Whatever It Takes! - Go For It! - Trust God - Take One Step And God Will Take Two For You and another Surrender To Win. Above the door on the other side of the room was a sign that read, Follow the path down to your next set of instructions. You will receive further instructions upon your arrival.

The door to this room led us to a wide open space on top of a hill that over-looked a very dense jungle. I had to stop and remind myself that I was on the first floor in a building on the east side of town. From our vantage point we looked down into a green valley and the sun was slowly going down. A narrow winding path led down into the valley and disappeared into a jungle of tall trees and shrubbery. Each side of the path was lined with shrubbery that stood at least 10 feet high. A heavy mist hovered over one part of the valley that covered what appeared to be a lake of some kind. Strange sounds echoed throughout the valley as huge birds circled above. It was as if the birds were on patrol protecting every inch of this crazy looking valley.

As we stood at the door looking down into this valley, some members of our group hesitated and considered not continuing out of fear. Someone said that it didn't look safe and that they wanted to wait for more instructions. We tried to talk them into coming with us, but fear paralyzed them, keeping them from moving. Twelve of us, including Janet, Shorty and Carmen began this hike down into the jungle while the rest of the group stood at the top of the hill contemplating what to do next. Shorty said "this wasn't here the last time I came through this building."

The farther we walked down into the jungle, the thicker the shrubbery became and the path narrowed. We were about one hundred yards down into the valley when we could no longer see our friends who were at the top of the hill. The path had gotten constricted with shrubbery and as soon as it looked like we could not go any farther, we came to a clearing where we found a large sign at the edge of the lake, and it read, "Take Alternate Path". An arrow pointed us towards another path that led back towards the building we just left, but we ended up on the back side.

We all followed this path to another door that led us into another room. There were chairs in this room where we all took a seat. A woman came out to greet us. She introduced herself as Quianna. Quianna was a tall blonde with curly short hair and tattoos on both of her arms and one on her ankle. She had an attractive face and a nice smile. First she applauded us for being willing to take the next step. Then she began to share her life story with us and how she made it through the room called WILLINGNESS. She said "now that you have started this process called recovery you have to start trusting others and learn how to take directions from others.

You also have to be willing to go to any lengths to be free from our addiction. You that were willing to go down into the valley passed a very simple test, a test that you will have to continue to take while in recovery. You are now ready to move on to the next room". Janet said, "Is that it?" Quianna laughed and said, "That is the same thing I said when I came made it out this room. Here, in the "WILLINGNESS" room, all you have to do is be willing. In life you will find if you take one step, God will take two for you. In life some things will be foreign to you. You will have to participate even when you do not want to.

Many travel down the road of life and because of fear they leave five minutes before the miracle takes place. They are tricked by Satan, who uses fear and scare tactics, to discourage them from advancing to the next level. A great way to overcome these fears is to spend time in the room called "CHANGE" and learn how to voice your fears and concerns. In these rooms, you will hear your story and recognize you are not alone. In these rooms, you will learn to share your fears, feelings and your experiences amongst people who are just like you. In the room call "CHANGE" you have to learn to trust others that have been through the process call recovery and have traveled down the same road you are attempting to travel. This is where you will learn trust totally in God. The will to be honest and the will to change are signs of a great start for anyone who wants to be free.

We left the room, and Quianna led us down a hall that took us to another room. As we arrived at the next room, there was a large glass mirror on the wall. After all twelve of us made it into the room, Quianna turned the lights off, and we could now see people on the other side of the mirror, but they could not see us. To our surprise, it was our friends who decided not to follow us down into the valley. They continued to stand at the door called "WILLINGNESS" still afraid to go down the path. As I looked through the glass, I could see the t-shirts that they were wearing, that read, "God will never leave you or forsake you." I thought to myself this must be what trust is all about. We have to believe that everything will be all right no matter what.

I asked Quianna "what will happen to those individuals who did not move on with us. Quianna said, "Some eventually go through the doors of "WILLINGNESS" and continue on in the process of recovery. Some stay in the room and eventually go back to the basement, while others leave the building all together." Quianna also said not to worry about them, because God is still in charge of their lives just as He is in charge of yours. At that moment, I saw Ronnie, the salesman, standing at the door of "WILLINGNESS". I tried to get his attention by tapping the glass and yelling to him, but he could not hear me. It was hard to believe Ronnie was still there.

If Ronnie fails to complete this program, the judge will send him back to jail. Quianna told me that I was powerless, and, Ronnie, like the rest of them, would have to make up their minds to take that initial step towards a better life, just like everyone else.

So, now, there were only 12 of us left. We, being, Janet, Shorty, Carmen, Bobby, a 39-year- old construction worker who still lives with his mom, Nyna, the dancer, Dennis the truck driver, Keith the house painter, Rodney the computer operator, Hazel the stay-at-home mom, Wendell the actor, Annette the college administrator, and myself. We had just gotten started and we had lost some people already. As Quianna led us down another hallway, I had never felt so helpless in all of my life. I wanted everyone to make it through recovery, but, at the same time, I knew I had to make it myself before I could help anyone else.

We came upon another table that had more t-shirts stacked on top of it. The sign above the table read "Take one shirt and put it on." The inscription on the shirt read, "DON'T LEAVE 5 MINUTES BEFORE THE MIRACLE."

While walking out of the room, some questioned what we had gotten ourselves into by entering *Recovery Tower*. For me, what I had witnessed was far better than where I came from. To be honest, I was looking forward to what was next. It was surely better than getting paid on Friday and being broke the next day.

The next room was called HONESTY & ACCEPTANCE. Once we walked into this room, we noticed twelve doors that led to other rooms. Signs and posters again lined the walls of the room. The first one read "One of the biggest enemies of the recovering person is his distorted thinking and deceitful lifestyle". Another sign read, "To thine own self be true." Another read, "Don't be a fake, phony and fraud." I thought to myself "what is this all about"? We were all led to one of 12 doors. I noticed my name posted on the door in front of me.

As I walked into the room, the lights came on. To my surprise, this room was an exact replica of my old apartment. Everything was the same - from the pictures on the wall to the books on the shelves - to the furniture in the living room, even the color of the paint in the kitchen, and the layout of the den, was exactly the same. As I walked into the bedroom, my TV and stereo system was in the same place. This was starting to feel weird, like something out of the "Twilight Zone". As I walked in front of my bedroom mirror, I noticed the writings on my t-shirt, DON'T LEAVE 5 MINUTES BEFORE THE MIRACLE! Reading those words could not have come at a better time, because, in my past something this spooky I would have left 10 minutes ago! The saying on the shirt was a reminder for me to stay and trust in this process that was not out to hurt me, but for my ultimate good. I had to also remember what I learned in the room called "Willingness". Put one foot in front of the other and trust God!

It took me a while to get used to my surroundings; nevertheless, I settled in and moved around this apartment as if it were really mine. I did, however, notice one thing that was different. There was food in the refrigerator and in the cabinets. That rarely happened in my apartment. I could not remember the last time I went shopping. I only got food for that moment or that day. After eating and enjoying a little cable TV, I decided to turn in for the night. After all, it had been a long and somewhat unusual day. I sat back in my lounge chair and dozed off.

I began to dream about my young adult days while in high school, which were some very trying times for me. The dream began with the pressures of trying to fit in and be a part of the "in" crowd and how hard that was. My dad use to tell me that I was a people pleaser. I disagreed with him. I just wanted to be accepted like other kids. Next the dream showed me finding a home in sports, where I played football, baseball, basketball, and ran track. The dream then took me back to my fist touchdown pass that won the game against our cross-town rivals. It showed the home runs I hit in different baseball games, the great defensive plays I made that helped us to win ball games. My name was in the local paper as an up and coming star. In the dream, I talked to the scouts that came out to the games to watch me play and all the letters I received from different colleges that wanted to recruit me.

Next, this dream shifted to my college years where I partied and stayed in nightclubs all night long, and, because of that life style, I was always cramming for tests or barely beating deadlines. In the dream, I saw vividly the girls who chased me. I was a playboy on campus and always hung out with the popular crowd. Anytime there was a party or a function, I was invited and I was always there.

Next, the dream moved on into the days after college, where I walked away from all the good that was taught to me as a kid, and I started smoking and selling drugs. I thought I could out-smart the world by making illegal money, meeting and hanging out with the players and hustlers! This was the life I wanted to live before I became hooked on the very drugs I was selling.

I woke up that next day pretty well rested. As I ate breakfast, I started thinking about the dream I had the night before, but I didn't put too much into it because it was a dream. I was still trying to figure out why I was here in an apartment that resembled the apartment I used to live in and what did it have to do with this room called HONESTY & ACCEPTANCE.

I had been in this room over fourteen hours and nothing made any sense. After lunch, I turned on the radio and I could only receive one station. I was instructed to pull up a chair in front of the TV. Then, I was instructed to pick up the remote control. The remote was different from any other remote I had ever seen. There were four buttons: power on and power off, true, and false. I hit the "power on" button and the television screen turned white. Seconds later a replay of the dream from the night before began playing.

It showed me in high school, and then a message appeared. The words true or false flashed on the screen. I pushed the True button, and the story of my life resumed. I saw again the days when I played football. The words true or false flashed across the screen again, and, again, I pushed the true button and the story of my life continued to play on. It was the final game of the season: I caught the pass that won the biggest game of the year against our cross-town rivals. Again, true or false flashed on the screen. I hit true. The screen lit up and began to flash false – false - false and a voice came through the speakers on the TV and said, "To Thine Own Self Be True". Wow! I didn't need four years of college to see what was going on. I sat back in the chair knowing that this room was about to get serious.

This room was going to make me get honest. I'd been living this football lie for a long time. I never caught the winning pass to win any game. I caught a couple of passes in regular season games, but none of them were game winners. I have been telling that lie for years, so much so that I started believing it. I looked back at the TV screen and the words continued to flash false – false. I grabbed the remote and hit the button that said false, and the dream continued to play.

The next screen showed me hitting a home run and then the videotape stopped and displayed on the monitor: "True or False". I pushed the True button and the video continued on. Next, it showed me getting these letters from different colleges to play ball with them and came to an abrupt halt again: True or false. I pushed true and it began to flash false - false and a voice said, "To Thine Own Self Be True". . I was on the team, but, certainly, I was in no way the star, nor had any colleges sent me any letters, nor had scouts tried to recruit me. Talk about busting my bubble… As I sunk down into my chair it was obvious "Frank needed to get honest with Frank". I immediately hit false, and my continued to play out before me.

This dream I had the night before was now becoming a night mare on this 32-inch TV screen. Slowly it began to peel away the layers of deceit and lies in my life. The video moved quickly to my first year in college. At that time, I really enjoyed the "college life" and everything that went along with it. I loved the whole college environment, hanging out, going to parties, staying up all night and cramming for tests. The dream stopped and the screen flashed again True or False? I hesitated and thought about what was going on here during this period of my life. I began thinking back and trying to be as honest as I possibly could. We did party a lot and my friends and I did cram for tests, so I pressed "True". My dream continued to play out and being honest wasn't as easy as one would think.

Next it went into a period of my life that I thought would have been easy telling the truth, but I was soon to find out not so!

The screen moved into my dealing with the opposite sex. From high school to college I thought I was a pretty good ladies man, so I pushed the button true and, again, the words on the monitor flashed false – false and again the voice came from the TV "To Thine Own Self Be True". I got up out of my chair and tossed the remote to the floor. "This thing has to be broken," I thought. At this time, the TV began playing in reverse and then it stopped. It started playing my real life and actual situations dealing with some of the women that I had been intimate with.

As I sat back down in the chair, an instant replay showed me at night clubs chasing women, trying to be the ladies man. One of the tools that I used that was consistent with all of the women I dated, or tried to date, was consuming alcohol and using drugs in all my encounters. Alcohol gave me the courage to approach many of the women I sought and I always tried to keep their glasses full. I sunk down deeper in the chair and faced the fact that 99.9 percent of the time I had to use alcohol or some mind-altering chemical in order for me to have my way with the women I met. What a sobering moment.

This HONESTY room had now busted a bubble that I really didn't want busted. What kind of man did this really make me? Was I afraid to let women know who I really was, or did I even know who I really was? Who was the real Frank? It was obvious to me that I did not like who I was. I drank to become someone other than the real me. Once I took a drink I was "that guy" fast talking hip, slick, and a cool ladies man. Finally, my life story was back to the question, "Was I a ladies man?" True or false flashed before me. I picked up the remote off of the floor and pushed the "False" button. What a fake I thought my entire life is a fake. It's all a lie.

After being stripped down to nothing, I realized I was no more than a man who was not living an honest life at all. It was merely a figment of my imagination. I couldn't even sell drugs right, hell I ended up becoming my best customer. What a failure. What was I going to do for the rest of my life, where do I begin? It's a hard thing to swallow that you've been a fake, phony, and fraud for most of your life.

This was too much I was ready to leave the HONESTY & ACCEPTANCE ROOM. It was getting late and the thought of going to sleep and facing another dream was too much to bear. I still had a lot of my life to review, so I purposely stayed up forcing myself not to go to sleep, but I couldn't stop it from happening and dosed off.

There was no let up; the dream examined every part of my life. The next day I made up my mind to push the "False" button, for everything. That would have been easier than going through the pain of facing the real me. My middle name should be chameleon because I made every part of my life better than what it was.

Once the dream finished playing out in front of me, and my ego was smashed flatter than a dime, a sign on the TV screen read "To Thine Own Self Be True". "To Thine Own Self Be True".   Depression consumed me. Feeling miserable, I sat on the edge of the bed when the doorbell rang. It was Quianna. She could see that I had been beaten up pretty bad. Quianna led me into the kitchen and began making coffee. I took a seat and she explained why honesty was so important in order to change. She then said there is no such thing as an honest addict/alcoholic, they do not exist. If they are not deceiving the people around them, they are deceiving themselves. <u>Deceit is a necessary component to keep those addicted in bondage.</u> In the beginning, we lie to ourselves trying to hold on to the images we create of ourselves.

Aside whatever environment we grew up in, addicts have certain visions of what they want out of life. Once an addict begins to lose sight of his or her dreams due to their drug and alcohol abuse, he or she lives in a state of constant denial and begins to act as if their life, dreams, and expectations are still attainable.

Casual drinkers and users unknowingly cross the line into addiction and they cannot control their actions after that first drink or hit. The addictions creates a monster in side you that cannot be satisfied

(One hit is too many and a thousand never enough). You become a full-blown addict/alcoholic, and your goal now, is to hide the monster that is now in control of your life. No one must know that you are out of control, so you do all you can to protect the image that you believe you still have. Unbeknownst to you, most of your family, friends, and those who work with you know that you have a problem. It is impossible to be a practicing alcoholic/addict, without becoming a liar, cheat, a fake, phony and fraud. It is impossible for those close to you not to know or be affected by your drinking and using.

Most of the time, the addicted person is the last one to recognize they have a problem. Many people struggling with this disease have lost jobs, and their family members have washed their hands of them and will, literally, have nothing to do with them. Sometimes devastating things has to happen to the addicted person before he or she finally takes a look at him or herself. People who work in recovery call it "hitting a bottom", or "crashing and burning".

From the housewife, who is addicted to prescription medication, to the everyday drunk who is homeless and living on the street, deception is a big part of their lives. Some may call it "telling little white lies" or "bending the truth". Others call it survival, but lying is part of the life of all practicing addicts/alcoholic. These lies become habits that alter your behavior, and addict/alcoholic lying to cover up previous lies they told. As I sat there and listened, all I could say was "ouch" as Quianna continued hammering me with this truth.

She continued as we both sip coffee. "Some of us become chameleons so to speak. You could drop them into any situation and they will adapt by telling you what you want to hear. These individuals cannot be trusted in any way, shape, or form because they are selfish, self centered, and will do whatever it takes to take care of themselves, even if it means hurting others. A chameleon can adapt to any situation and be whatever you want him or her to be, in this case, in order to get what he or she desires. They are experts at "fitting in" and, within no time, they will examine a situation and become the answer to that situation by deceiving everyone involved. What usually happens to this person is he or she eventually deceives themselves. By the time this individual makes it to the rooms of recovery, they do not have the slightest idea who they are.

Quianna shared how important it is to start building a new foundation with a clean slate. When erecting a building, the last thing you want to do is build it on a cracked foundation. In the beginning of recovery, it is necessary that you be honest with yourself, or how else can you ever be honest with another human being or God? Remember, you are on the first floor. This is the beginning, and you cannot start this process of recovery living a lie. Those who try to continue living this lie experience unnecessary hardship and pain; therefore, they never move freely through the recovery process. These individuals go through the motions of being free, but they end up carrying baggage that gets heavier as the recovery process gets deeper.

"FAKES, PHONYS, and FRAUDS" are what they become - struggling through life, never enjoying peace, joy, nor serenity. Most of them end up returning to the pain and suffering that brought them to recovery in the first place. To these types of individuals, we say "Good Luck"; instead of "Be blessed" you're going to need it. You have to let go and let God.

She then got up and began walking towards the door. Before leaving she turned and said "Make up your mind today on how you want to live your life for the rest of your life. Free to grow by leaps and bounds in this new life of recovery, or bound by deceit; always looking over your shoulder making sure you do not stumble over a lie that you have created in your past, and she tuned and left. I returned to the kitchen thinking about everything that had happen in these last few days. As I finished my coffee I thought about what Quianna shared. It made sense to start fresh, with a clean slate. The only problem was I didn't know if I'd be able to distinguish between what was right and what was wrong.

As I headed for the door to exit the apartment, feeling lower than I had ever felt, I was hit with another gut-wrenching blow - there was a sign on the door that read, "Who is the real Frank?" After thinking about this question for a few minutes, I could not come up with an answer. I put my head down and walked out of the apartment which ironically became too real and closed the door behind me. I had become a fake, phony, and fraud. I looked down the hallway and everyone seemed to be exiting at the same time. There was pure silence in that hallway, and the blank look on everyone's face ranged from unbelief, guilt and sorrow.

Shorty walked up to me and asked me if I was all right. I tried to smile and said, "I think so," I asked him if he was okay and he laughed and said, "Yeah, it was even tougher the second time around." I had forgotten Shorty had been here before. He said the first time, he really did not want to believe the image of himself that was played out before him, but this time he was willing to do whatever it took to recover completely. I, then, told him that I admired his courage to come back into the building and start again. The honesty room had been a tough room, and I wondered what was next.

We were led down a long hallway; the silence gave me a chance to think about the time I wasted trying to be something I was not.

Again, we were led to the room called "CHANGE". I really needed to get in touch with these feelings I was experiencing. People began dumping all the garbage that they had been carrying around with them for years. While listening to everyone who went before me, I realized that I had not heard such sincere sharing in all my life. I was only on the first floor, yet I knew that I was going in the right direction. This time I raised my hand. I did not want to wait on someone to call on me. Still afraid, I turned and told my peers that I was afraid. I was afraid of this new life that I was getting ready to embark upon. I had no clue what was going to happen, but I was convinced anything was better than what I had and where I had come from. I also shared that I was tired of being a fake, phony, and a fraud. That was enough of being honest for me, and then I sat down.

Back To School

Can You Teach A Old Dog New Tricks?

Second Floor

It took me two months on the first floor to process all that I learned and figure out how it applies to my life. The "Honesty" part was the hardest, but the more willing I became, the easier the process of recovery looked to me. I started seeing the process work, and 2 months without drinking and using was a miracle.

We moved on to the second floor, convinced that the lessons learned on the first floor would be something we would have to apply to our lives for the rest of our lives.

Once we entered the elevator, and the doors closed behind us, a voice came over the intercom saying, "Remember that the road to recovery is a process and complete healing will not come overnight. It took years to get to this point, so it is going to take some time to be restored back to sanity." Sanity! "So now, they think I'm insane or crazy. Who do they think they are? I admit to having a drug problem, but being crazy, wait just a minute." I was insulted and offended by this. Janet looked at me and said "why would anyone think that I was crazy"? I told Janet "maybe I'm in the wrong place, maybe it's time for me to leave this weird building". To my surprise, Shorty looked at me and said, "Stop tripping, if you drank or used anything like me, you put drinking and using before everything. You needed drugs or alcohol to get you going in the morning, to make it through the day and something to put you to sleep!" I got paid on Friday and was broke by Saturday morning, now if that isn't crazy what is"?

A hush went through the elevator and after thinking about it, I had to agree that my behavior was insane. Why would a person almost lose their life doing drugs and, then, turn around and buy more? My way of life was insane. I could not believe that in a moment I had forgotten everything and my pride had me thinking about leaving. What is wrong with me I thought? People have said far worse things to me on the street and in the dope houses. Their words never bothered me at all as long as I got my dope. Young dope dealers talked about me like I was nothing because I was a few dollars short after giving them my whole check. Now, all of a sudden, I cannot seem to handle the truth and I am ready to turn and run. I thanked Shorty for bringing me back to earth and I was ready to continue.

A sign on the elevator door read: "Those who try and hurry through this process without using these tools tend to repeat the process by returning to the bottom." We called these people chronic relapsers.

When the doors to the elevator opened, there was an attendant standing there to meet us. He introduced himself as Isaiah. Isaiah was a tall thin man with red hair. Smiling he asked us, "Are you having fun yet?" We all looked at him as if he were crazy. He told us not to get discouraged and that God did not bring us this far to leave us. "What comforting words, I thought". Isaiah, then, led us down another hall and through a door that led us to an outside area. Annette the college administrator lean over to me and said, "Are we still inside the building"? Laughing I told her "There cannot be anything on the east side that looks like this". We were standing on what looked like a train station platform, but there was no train in sight. There were railroad tracks on the ground in front of us that disappeared around a bend that was about 50 feet ahead of us. Behind us, the tracks disappeared into a fog bank about 50 feet from us - the fog looked like a blanket that hovered in one spot and did not come any closer. Suddenly, in the distance, we heard a rumbling sound coming towards us. Each second brought the sound closer. We all stood there looking into the fog bank. Suddenly a transparent glass monorail train emerged from the fog bank and eased its way up to the platform where we stood. A group of people were already on board the train. Once the train came to a complete stop, the passengers all got out of their seats and exited the train. We, the faithful 12, then boarded the monorail and took our seats. There was only one seat on either side of the train separated by an aisle. Isaiah told us to fasten our seatbelts and hold on tightly.

Slowly, the monorail began to pull away from the station. I wondered where in the heck we were headed now. Once the monorail made it to the Bend in the track, Isaiah picked up a microphone and told us to hold on. The monorail began to climb upward and picked up momentum. We traveled higher and faster so much so that the force pinned us to our seats. We continued accelerating at this speed for about 5 minutes when all of a sudden the monorail began to level out and slow down. We were so high up that we could barely see the ground. Right above us was a blanket of clouds that stretched out as far as the eye could see. We were cruising around 50 mph right below a group of scattered clouds when suddenly a white package shot right past my window. It seemed as though this package came from below, passed the monorail, and zoomed through the clouds right above us.

The train slowed up and slowly moved at about 10 mph. Several wrapped packages shot by the monorail, and they disappeared through the clouds above us. One package bounced off the clouds and fell back to earth. More and more packages were coming from the ground. Because we were in this glass monorail, we could see it happen all around us. Most of these packages were going through the clouds, but some were bouncing off the clouds and returning to the ground.

The monorail finally came to a stop and, all around us; these packages were shooting through the clouds with no end in sight. Some of us got out of our seats to get a better look.

Everyone on the monorail was dying for answers as Isaiah began to speak. He said "What you are witnessing are prayers going up to God". Everyone's eyes got as big as quarters. Hazel, the stay-at-home mom shouted from the back of the train, "Is God above these clouds?" "Yes." Isaiah answered and a hush went through the monorail. Those who were standing quickly took their seats, as if they were going to get into trouble or something. I could not speak for everyone else, but I was nervous. I looked up through the glass ceiling of the monorail and wondered what was going on up there on the other side of the clouds. I wondered what God was doing. Did He know we were here? What did He look like? Did He know I was asking these questions?

Isaiah explained why some prayers made it through the clouds and some did not. "Most prayers make it through, but only God makes the decision to answer those prayers. *Jesus is the way the truth and the life. No one comes to the Father but by Him.* Bottom line there is order in the Kingdom of Heaven. Jesus receives each prayer and presents them to God the Father".

Bobby, the construction worker, raised his hand to ask a question and Isaiah pointed to him and said, "In all due respect to God", as he looked through the top of the glass monorail, "and please don't get me wrong, I really don't want to offend Him. I am happy God came to my rescue, but I did not say in Jesus name when I called on him standing before that judge that was about to give me 10 years in prison. I just said, God, Will You Please Help Me?" Most of us smiled because most of us agreed. Isaiah, then, said "God knew the day in which you would surrender; God is answering the prayers of someone that has been praying for you! Think back when you were growing up, who was praying for you? Your mother, your father, grandparents who was it? Maybe God is answering their prayers.

That was easy for me to figure out it was my mother and my grandparents that prayed for me. That had to be it, God was honoring their prayers. I can remember spending weekends with my grandparents and them dragging me to church. I can remember getting sick as a child and my grandparents praying for me. That had to be the beginning of God doing for me in spite of me.

As I looked out into this vast space watching these prayers land at the feet of God I could not help but wonder if I could put my trust in God the way these people were trusting Him.

Wendell, the actor who was sitting in the seat in front of me, raised his hand and asked, "Why are some prayers not making it through to God?" Isaiah smiled and said, "That is a hard question to answer, but some prayers don't line up with God's will for that person's life, and, still, others are selfish prayers. Some of you prayed to God to rid yourself of the addiction, but you really wanted God to the remove you from the situation you were in at that time so you could continue drinking and using.

The monorail began to move and Isaiah told us to fasten our seat belts again. Descending through the hundreds of prayer requests that continued to bombard heaven, the monorail moved through the clouds with blinding speed. As we approached our destination, the monorail decreased in speed considerably. We were now sitting on top of a thick layer of clouds, just like the ones we had just left, but this time we were above the clouds.

The monorail moved slowly until it came to a halt on top of a sheet of glass. Through the floor of the monorail, we could see that the glass we were resting on was some sort of magnifying glass. This magnifying glass gave us a close up of people praying. It also pierced through buildings and we could see those individuals who were sending up the prayers. We could see people sending up prayers up close and personal. I saw a little girl about eleven years old walking to school, praying and talking to God. Then, I saw a mailman going from house to house praying while delivering his mail. Next, I saw a grandmother on her knees inside of her house praying. A man drove by in his car praying. I saw a church service that generated many prayers. In other words, I saw regular people talking to God at any time. This was new to me I only talked to God when I was in trouble or when my mother made me go to church as a kid.

Isaiah explained, "We go to God because He is our Father, because He loves us and He wants to hear from us. Prayer is how we communicate with Him." Then Isaiah said something that will stick with me forever. He said, "Those who choose not to pray trust in them self. Whatever your reason for not praying, your actions speak loud and clear saying, "You do not need God." Wow I thought that was deep.

The monorail began to move slowly as everyone sat there digesting everything we had seen and heard. The monorail went into another dive and within minutes, we were back where we started. When the doors opened, there was another group standing on the platform ready to take our places. As one guy walked by, we smiled at each other. He said to me, "How was it?" as he stepped onto the monorail, and I replied, "PRAY BROTHER, PRAY".

After exiting the monorail we were met by another instructor. Her name was Holly. Holly looked like a hippie of the late 60's, with beads around her neck and wrist wearing baggie jeans with a flower in her hair. She led us down a hall, and I overheard Janet and Carmen talking as they walked behind me. Janet said to Carmen, "Can you believe all of this is in a twelve-story building?" I turned and looked at them in disbelief, because I had forgotten where we were. We were led to another set of doors and Holly turned and said, "Your journey on the second floor continues, enter and enjoy."

We walked into a room that had twelve booths along the wall. These booths looked bigger than voting booths, but were smaller than recording studio booths. As we stood there wondering what was going on, Holly told us that this room is where we were to begin developing our personal relationships with God. In this room, we would learn how to send our prayers up to God. She said it was very simple; all we had to do was start our prayer with "In The Name Of Jesus," and be sincere when we talk to Him. She told us that in order for us to continue traveling in this building we had to begin developing a personal relationship with God. As I approached the booth, I could see that it had a cushion on the floor for those that preferred to kneel and a chair for those that wanted to sit. Holly could tell that some of us were having problems with this. I could not speak for everyone else, but this was foreign to me. As Holly left the room, she told us not to be afraid, and that God was not only our Father, but our friend. She continued encouraging us and, then, she looked at me and said, "Just keep it real."

We all stepped into our booths and an uneasy feeling came over me. I knew God was real, but I really did not know how to approach Him. I knew my grandparents had a relationship with God, because they talked about Him all the time while growing up. Every summer, we would go and visit them and you could feel this presence when you walked in their home. I also knew that they talked to God on my behalf, but I never thought this is how I would start my journey with Him.

I thought about our monorail ride and how some prayers went up through the clouds and some did not. I surely wanted God to hear me so I had already made up my mind to start and end my prayers with, "In the name of Jesus". It was what I was going to say in the middle that had me worried. I remembered what Holly said, "Keep It Real."

I got down on my knees and closed my eyes, "In the name of Jesus," God please forgive me for being such an idiot. I am tired of living the way I had been living, and if you can't help me, I'm in big trouble. Please keep the drugs and alcohol away from me and remove the taste out of my mouth. Please help me to know you better and last but not least please don't get mad at me if I messed up."

I prayed for my family and for all those whom I hurt and let down in my life. I prayed for my new friends who were taking this journey with me. I prayed that we would all succeed and get better as we go through this program. I ended the prayer "In Jesus' Name" and got off my knees.

I stood there wondering if that was too short of a prayer, or if there was a time limit on prayer itself. Then, I wondered if my prayers bounced off the clouds and came back to earth, or had they landed at the feet of God?

When I walked out of the door, I was surprised to see that some of my friends had just finished praying and were waiting for the rest of us to join them. I knew I had to spend more time with God, but this was a first for me and I wanted to keep it real. I had already learned on the first floor that I was a fake, a phony, and a fraud, and I didn't want to bring that behavior into this new life.

Holly led us back to the room called "CHANGE", where we each took a seat and the idea of prayer and having a relationship with the Lord was on the lips and minds of everyone. Finally, Nyna, the dancer, approached the podium. She introduced herself as a recovering addict and asked the question that I was afraid to ask simply because I did not want anyone to know that I knew nothing about God. She asked, "How can God love me after the way I've lived?" I think Nyna asked this question because she was a stripper. She shared for a few more minutes, and then took her seat.

The next person to speak at the podium was Dennis, the truck driver who introduced himself as a recovering alcoholic and a sex addict. Dennis was also the son of a preacher and knew a lot about the Word of God. He said "God called me to preach a long time ago, but I've been running from God most of my life. I hated being a preacher's kid and I hated how people always expected me to be like my father. I got a problem with the people in the church because I seen how my father would bend over backwards for them and they would turn around and stab him in the back!" It was easy to see that Dennis was very angry and had deep-rooted resentments with this whole religious thing. After a few minutes of venting, the preacher came out in him. He said "with all the things that he had seen and all the things he had done, he still believed in and loved God even in my madness". He then, answered Nyna's question. He said, "God is our creator, so He knows all about us. He never stopped loving us even in our sin, and it was because of that love that we are here in this building today. God loves us so much that He gave His life for us."

After Dennis finished, we were off to another room. Before we entered the room, Holly told us to get into a circle and grab each other's hands. Isaiah, then, prayed for all twelve of us calling each of us by name.

When he finished praying, a door in that room opened and, we all walked into a valley filled with books. The hills and the mountains were filled with books. The trees and leaves were made of books. The clouds were formed in the image of books. Books were everywhere you looked. As far as the eye could see, there was nothing but books. Every book that had ever been written had to be here in this valley.

Far off in the distance, we could see a bright beam of light, shinning down in what looked like the middle of the valley. Holly then told us to "Head towards the light, and all roads lead to the light! She then told us to choose any book of your choice, and it is ours to keep." She smiled and closed the door. Carmen looked over at Janet rolling her eyes saying, "Looks like another adventure". We all laughed and made our way down into the valley.

After about a quarter mile into the valley we came to a point in the road that branched off into many directions. At the fork in this road, we found a sign that read, "All roads lead to the Light. Choose which is best for you." A street sign described what type of road we could travel. One sign read: "Spiritual Disease of Addiction," and another read: "Codependency," and another read: "What is recovery?" and another sign read: "Powerlessness." A large sign in the middle of all these signs read "As long as you are in this building you can return to this point at any time and choose another road."

I along with Keith, Annette, and Rodney, selected the road called "Spiritual Disease of Addiction" while others chose other roads. Carmen told me she was going down the road called "Powerlessness". She was still having problems comprehending the powerless concept. After we said our goodbyes, we started down the road called "Spiritual Disease of Addiction." "Can your spirit be sick?" Rodney asked. Quickly we all started finding and picking up books to read. I noticed a book titled Addiction: Another Cancer. Once I picked up the book, I was surprised when another book with the same name appeared in its place. After we all found a book or two of our choice, we decided to take a break. So, we each found a tree to rest under and began to read the books we found.

In the book "Another Cancer", I was amazed to find out that most medical associations considered addiction to be a disease or sickness while Christian psychologists believe addiction to be a spiritual disease, some even calling it a sin-sick disease. The author said that alcoholism or any mind-altering addicted drug is like a cancer. Once the addiction has been diagnosed, treatment for the disease must begin immediately.

Without treatment, the disease gets progressively worse. With continued treatment, the addiction can go into remission and arrested as long as the individual continues taking the medicine (using the tools) that help them to find freedom.

Since the addiction lies dormant inside each recovering person, the recovering person has lost the right to socially drink and use again. They also have to steer clear of any "traps" or "triggers" that would lead them back to their former lifestyle.

On the other hand, those who do not treat addiction as a sickness stand a very good chance of this sickness returning to its initial, active state. For example, telling a person not to cough will not stop that person from coughing. In order for the cough to cease, that person has to take cough medicine, which will get to the crux of the issue that makes the individual cough.

Like treating any sickness, we must take medicine for our healing. For this spiritual sickness, we must use spiritual medicine. The author also said that spiritual disease is centered in the mind, so the goal of most counselors in this field should concentrate on renewing the mind. This is where the process of recovery comes in. At the same time, the mind never forgets this negative period of the recovering person's past. The mind never forgets the effects that were associated with each mind-altering chemical. The human mind never forgets the taste of the substances and liquor, nor the activities and the people who they were involved with while using.

It is recorded by recovering addicts and alcoholics with years of being clean and sober that dreams were so real that they thought they'd relapsed. The Bible defines recovery in Romans 12:2 *"And be not conformed to this world: but be ye transformed by the renewing of your mind, that ye may prove what is that good, and acceptable, and perfect, will of God."*

On the other hand those in the anonymous program renew the mind by continuous meeting. They replace the old thinking with new information.

It is clear that some addicts and alcoholics are sicker than others, but once the line into addiction is crossed, one cannot go back to sociable consumption. The door has been forever closed. This is the hardest truth for many addicts/alcoholics to accept. A person that drank and used and abused for 5, 10, 15 – 20 years, their sickness is deeper and more involved than a person with less time. The relationship with the drugs or alcohol is more intense, and to sever ties is like losing a friend.

If a person has a cold, pneumonia, or the flu, is it possible that he or she has a little cold, a little pneumonia, or just a little flu? Some would say, "Yes" but most would say, "No," you either have a cold or you don't, you are either sick or you are not. The day that you are diagnosed with the disease of addiction, you will need a power greater than yourself to relieve you of the pain caused by the sickness.

One chapter in this book is called "Spiritual Mind Cleansing", and it talks about renewing the mind with the things of God. Throwing out the bad and replacing it with new thoughts is one method of, literally, renewing the mind. Some say it is a nice way of saying brain washing. As I sat there and thought about all the stupid things I did under the influence.

Years of wasting my life away drinking and using and all the money I wasted on drugs and alcohol, my brain, honestly, needed washing.

Finally, this book made it clear to me that I was not a bad person trying to become good, but a sick person who was trying to become well. That idea blew me away. Who knew? I have always wondered why after every attempt to quit using, something would draw me back to it. Like a bee drawn to honey, I could not resist the temptation. I had to have it. After every failed attempt, I would beat myself up. It was starting to get the best of me, and I was truly ready to give up all together. Now, to find out that I am a sick person and not an evil person is a big relief.

We read these books for a couple of hours and decided to continue towards the bright beaming light off in the distance.

At the end of each day, all roads led to a common area where we could eat, study, and get more rest. Of course, there was the room called "Change" and, so this was our first stop. It was great because we, the "twelve", were together again, and we had developed a special bond. I sat down next to Hazel and I asked her why she went down the road called "codependency". Hazel said "I was married to a heroin addict who had been free from his addiction for two years, but they were now separated. Hazel said "I did everything in my power to keep our family together and to hide his sickness. "In the last year of my husband's using, I couldn't take it any longer. I never knew if he would come home loaded or come home sick because he needed a fix or would he come home at all. Or was I going to get a call in the middle of the night saying he was in jail or overdosed somewhere. So I started drinking to kill the pain always waiting and hoping he would stop. Two years ago he came to a building similar to this one and once he got clean he couldn't handle my drinking and he left me! This made me drink even more. My kids are grown and have lives of their own, and the bad part about it I still love my husband.

Hazel was reading a book titled: Loved ones and Friends, the #1 Enemy to the Recovering Person. She also had another book called "Is Love Blind."

After the meeting in the room called "Change" we went to the room where they served food. After eating one of the best steaks I ever had Hazel sat down beside me with her face buried in one of the books. I don't think she stop to eat. Hazel began to read out loud to me some of passages she had underlined in the book. "Did you know that many practicing addicts and alcoholics prey on "normal" people with goals of winning them over?"

I just sat there and listen knowing deep down inside she was right because I was one of those people. This is how I was able to drink and use for so long, this is how I survived? Hazel was just coming to grips that she had been used by her husband and the look on her face was pure hurt. She continued there was a chapter in the book titled: In search of Weak Women, In search of Weak Men. She continued to read "Addicts and alcoholics looked for people, especially members of the opposite sex who may be lonely or have a caring and giving spirit.

An addict/alcoholics job is to win a person over. Committing to them in every way, saying I love you, means nothing to an addict/alcoholic. Remember they are liar, cheats and can't be trusted. They will do anything to support their habit!

Once the addicts have destroyed their own lives, they zero in on anyone that will believe them. People that take care of addicts or alcoholics are called codependents.

Codependents specialize in rescuing, and preventing addicts and alcoholic from falling, but what they end up doing is assisting them in their drinking and using. The codependent is the last one to know how much harm they are actually causing. Eventually, the addict/alcoholic destroys the codependent's life as well."

She then shares another passage. "The best place to find co-dependent people is in the church. "Been there done that" I thought! The alcoholic/addict, or predators, as the book referred to them, uses Church goers because of the love of God that resides inside of them.

Predators become experts at using the Word of God to gain the confidence of their victims. Once they have gained their trust, the addict or alcoholic cannot hide the disease any longer. The double life of being in the church and an alcoholic/addict is too much to carry. The Christian that they've deceived feels obligated to support them out of Christian love. Slowly the disease progresses and the addict/alcoholic destroys everything in their path. During this time they drag their loved ones and friends down with them.

Addicts and alcoholics become experts at giving empty promises leaving dreams unfulfilled; always ready to give another excuse, another lie. The addict/alcoholic looks for people in the church because they know Christians believe in love, forgiveness, mercy, and grace. The loved one or friend now becomes a cushion to break their fall. As Hazel continued to read tears rolled down her cheeks.

As I sat there and listened, I was consumed with guilt. I thought about the women that I had used and abused, the lies I had told and the money that I had taken knowing that I would never pay the money back. I allowed these women to take me to church and have the man of God pray for me, knowing that this was just a ploy to get me back into their lives. I would drink a can of "act right" for a while, but as soon as it wore off and they let their guard down, I would start drinking and using all over again. It was time to turn in and I wanted to pray with Hazel but I could not bring myself to ask her. So before hopping into bed I said a prayer for her.

That next morning after breakfast we could see that light beaming down not far from us. Some of use continued down the same path, while others changed paths. Once I finished the books, I was reading, I collected a few more in an attempt to get all the information I could.

After a couple of hours of reading, walking, and sharing, we finally arrived at a spot where a light was shining brightly. As we drew nearer, the light seemed to draw us closer to it. We could see that all the roads in the "land of books" led us to the light. All the roads came together, and the original twelve that started off together came back together once more. Once we arrived at the point where the light hit the ground, we could see that it was shining on one book in particular.

The book seemed to have a glow about it, and everyone did their best to see the name of this book. As we got closer, each of us saw that the book was THE HOLY BIBLE – THE BOOK OF ALL BOOKS. Everyone stood in line and picked up a Bible. Once we picked up a Bible, another appeared in its place. When I picked up my Bible, something inside me leaped. I had never had such a feeling. There was truly something very special about this book.

After we had retrieved our Bibles, a new instructor named Brice appeared and gathered us all together. Brice was a slim educated man with a Boston accent. He began to tell us the story of Jesus and His love for his people. He share that God loved us so much that He sent His only begotten Son to save a dying world. He talked about how God has another book called The Lambs Book of Life and the name of everyone who accepts Christ as his or her personal Lord and Savior is entered into this book. What blew my mind was God already knows who will accept Him and who will not. Another thing that I found fascinating was that God was taking care of me even when I did not know Him. This is evident by my being here in this building called *Recovery Tower*. Once I looked out the back door of my life, it was so easy to see that God brought me out of so many dangerous situations. Brice shared with us that soon we would all have an opportunity to accept Jesus Christ as our personal Lord and Savior and make Him Lord over our lives. As I looked around the room, I could feel some of my peers were ready to do it right then.

For a week, Brice walked us through the Bible and we went to the room call "Change" daily. There was so much to learn about God, recovery, and this new life. From what I could gather in this very short time, God was Holy, righteous, loving, and powerful. We stayed on the second floor of *Recovery Tower* for a total of two and a half weeks learning all that we could.

We left the world filled with books and headed back again to the room called "CHANGE". This day this room was very crowded. We found out that from here on out, people from all twelve floors would have access to the rooms called "CHANGE".

We, the faithful twelve, found seats in the room and turned our attention to the teacher in the front of the room. She identified herself as Rochelle. She was a tall, slim blonde and, at first glance, you would think she knew nothing about a drug or alcohol ravaged lifestyle; however, that was far from the truth. Rochelle told us that she supported her crystal-meth habit by embezzlement and money laundry. By looking at her, you would never suspect she was a recovering person.

Rochelle began by giving everyone the definitions of morality, truth, righteousness, and holiness. She said "these are the goals that we, in recovery, strive to obtain in our everyday lives." She describes these words as the foundation on which we build our newly-recovered life. "The higher you want to go in life, the deeper your foundation should be."

Rochelle spelled out the word B.I.B.L.E. - "Basic, Instruction, Before, Leaving, Earth." God knew that I needed some basic instructions. As Rochelle continued to share, I identified with her journey that drove her to get help. She said "I made a decision to change my life at a time when I really had no knowledge of God. One day, I had to make a decision to go forward with God or go back to my old lifestyle, and there is no in between. So I made up my mind to go all the way with God." I think this is the decision every person will have to make before growth can begin to take place. Going all the way with God seems like a lot, but as I looked back at my life anything was better than what I had.

After Rochelle finished speaking, she opened the floor for sharing. Shorty raised his hand and made his way to the podium. He shared about being teachable and being willing to change. He said "changing will be his biggest battle, but this time he would do his best to do this one day at a time". Shorty appeared to have so much knowledge. I really hoped that he would succeed this time. I began to think about the road ahead and what it would take to stay free from drugs and alcohol. Fear set in and my mind began to race, "What an order," I thought. "I've been living this way for such a long time." The sweat began to bead up on my forehead. I fought back against the thoughts of not making it and getting up and running out of this crazy building. Carmen must have noticed that I was having an anxiety attack or something, because she whispered in my ear "Like Shorty said we change one day at a time." I smiled and replied, "Some time, one minute at a time". A spirit of calm came over me. "One day at a time," made a lot of sense. Staying free from drugs and alcohol and living as a "Christian" for the rest of my life may seem unattainable, but staying free from drugs and alcohol and living as a "Christian" one day at a time, seemed very possible.

After Shorty finished speaking, it seemed like everyone had something to share. Some just wanted to talk about what we had been introduced to so far in this building of recovery. Annette asked, "Can you teach old dogs new tricks?" Everyone laughed, but if you think about it, it's not a bad question. I thought about it and decided that I had no other choice, but to "learn new tricks". After everyone had finished sharing, Rochelle returned to the podium and advised us to always remember to take advantage of the room called "CHANGE", because it is a big part of the medicine we will have to use. Here, we can talk about our fears, hopes, and feelings. She also told us that before we moved to the next floor, we had one more room to enter.

Rochelle was just about to dismiss us to go into the next room when she asked if anyone had a burning desire to share. I looked around the room and slowly raised my hand indicating my desire to share with the group and made my way to the podium. I told my peers that I was seriously thinking about turning my life over to God. Without knowing what all of that meant – judging by everything I had learned so far - I was convinced that God had a better plan for me than I had for myself. A smile lit up Rochelle's face and the people that worked in this building came in from everywhere clapping their hands and thanking and praising God. As I stood there, chills ran through my body. I was happy and I really was not sure why.

Another instructor named Lem walked in and started telling everyone in the room about the goodness of God. With a stern face, he looked me squarely into my eyes and said, "What you've decided to do is the most important decision you'll ever make in your entire life! Now that you decided to surrender your life to Christ, this does not mean that you have arrived and can stop working on yourself." He told me that many Christians return to drinking and using because they believe God is going to do the work for them now that they have accepted Christ into their lives. They stopped working on themselves believing they have found an easier and softer way to freedom. And like anyone who stops taking their medicine, eventually, they get sick and return to drinking and using. After his speech, everyone came up to me shaking my hand and patting me on the back. I was really thrown off by their reaction. "Why was everyone so happy?" For me, it was a decision I had to make, and I figured everyone else would do the same.

The faithful twelve were all assembled together, and we were led to another large room with twelve doors. The word "FAITH" was on every door. We were all told to go to a door and enter in whenever we were ready. I was not too anxious to enter this room after my experience in the Honesty and Acceptance Room.

After a slight hesitation, I turned the doorknob and entered in. Once inside, the door automatically closed behind me and the room was completely dark and I couldn't see anything. I ran my hand along the wall searching for a light switch, but I could not find one. I, then, tried to find the door handle, but there was no knob on the inside. As I stood there in the darkness, a voice came over an inter-com and said, "Darkness comes in many forms. When you were out there using and abusing, searching for a way out, this same fearful feeling came upon you." Afraid to move, I stood there for a few seconds wondering if I should knock on the door and maybe someone would hear me and let me out.

Finally, I took a step into the darkness and when I did, to my surprise, a panel lit up under my foot. So I took another step and another panel lit up. With each step, I got bolder, which gave me the courage to take more steps and lights began to shine all over the room. After a while, all the lights were on inside this room. On the other side of the room, there was a door that I could not see in the darkness. Above the door, there was a sign that read, "Faith Is an Action Word. Sometimes You Must Step Out Into Nothing To Receive Something". Another sigh read "God's Power Works Even When You Don't See It?"

I walked through the door and went back to the room called "CHANGE." Once we had taken our seats, another instructor name Sadie came to the podium. Before she could speak other instructors appeared from a back room with a cake filled with lit candles. Sadie was celebrating 26 years of complete abstinence from all mind altering substance. We all sung happy birthday and watched her blow out her candles.

Sadie said she was in her early 50's but you could tell by looking at her. She talked about having faith in the process even when it doesn't make any since. Millions of people are free from drugs and alcohol because of the Process of Recovery, so don't come in here changing anything.

She then said "give this new life a chance; what do you have to lose. If you don't like it we will gladly refund you misery right back to you." Some of us laughed, others looked shocked and still others didn't know how to feel. What she said was harsh but real.

She then said "many of you have been practicing faith and you didn't know it. When the dope man told you he'd be right back, faithfully you stayed there until he returned. Give yourself a break God has a better plan for you".

It was time to move on to the next floor. Before we left, Sadie reminded us that none of the doors we had to face could be opened without the tools we received on the first two floors. Then he said that there were no time limits in acquiring these very powerful tools, but without them, we could not proceed. Without them, we were destined to fail. Then she said "once we feel comfortable on this floor, we can move on to the next floor. Please take your time in this process called recovery. It took years to get sick; therefore, it will take years to be comfortable in your recover."

We walked down the hall towards the elevators that would take us to the third floor. We were surprised to see that there were now 12 individual elevators - one for each of us. We were going to be separated. Some faces showed fear, and then Annette said "I guess it's time to step out on faith we have to step out into nothing to land on something"

The doors opened to each elevator, and we all hopped on before the doors closed, Shorty shouted, "Don't leave 5 minutes before the miracle", as I stepped onto the elevator and turned towards the door that had just closed behind me. I notice the doors were made like a mirror and in my reflection I saw what my tee shirt read, "God will never leave you or forsake you ", and I said to myself, "Thank God for that."

Pretty sure no one proof-read this book before it was printed !!

Who Will You Serve
Make Up Your Mind

Third Floor

When the doors opened on the third floor, there was a huge welcome sign that read, "Welcome To Your Help and Your Help Comes From The Lord," underneath the sign, another sign read "Are You Ready to Change?" "There it is - that word again - "Change".

As I walked out of the elevator, a narrow cobblestone paved road navigated its way, down into a forest. On each side of the road, there were well-manicured bushes aligning the road. The sky was a royal blue and the sun positioned itself high in the sky as a gentle breeze blew through this area.

The road made its way to a large clearing, and in the center of the clearing, there were stairs with about 50 steps made out of white marble that lead up to a giant door that sat on a hill. The hand railing on the stairs was made out of solid brass, and the rails glistened in the sun as it led up to a giant door sitting at the top of the stairs. The door was not like any other door I'd seen while in this building. It was gold in color and stood at least fifty feet high. The molding and threshold around the door was laced in jewels. The sun's rays danced gently off each stone showing an array of colors that shined ever so brightly. Just looking at this door, I thought to myself that there was no way I would be able to open it, maybe there's a doorbell up there. As I stood at the bottom of the stairs, I wondered what or who could be behind this door?

Again remembering what happened to me on the 2nd floor, in the faith room, I made my way to the stairs that led to the large doors. I looked down on the marble steps. Engraved in the first step was written, "Choose You This Day Whom You Will Serve". After a few more steps, there were more inspirational writings. It read, "Do You Believe Jesus Died on The Cross for Your Sins, and, if you do believe, continue up the stairs." After a few more steps, there was even more writing. It read, "Do You Believe That God, The Father, raised Jesus from the Dead with All Power in His Hands?" If you do believe, continue up the stairs. The next set of steps read, "Do You Believe That Jesus Is the Son of God"? If you do believe, continue up the stairs. With my head down, looking at the next set of writings, it read, "Do You Accept Jesus Christ as Your Personal Lord and Savior?" If you do believe, continue walking up the stairs. I certainly believed and continued up the stairs. Tears began to run down my face, but I did not know why. With every step I took, a load seemed as if it was being lifted off of my shoulders. I looked to the heavens and whispered, "I believe".

Now, I was almost at the top of the stairs when a light shined upon me and the air became completely still. A peaceful voice came from above the clouds saying, "You have made the most important decision you will ever make in your entire life. Every angel in heaven is rejoicing because of your decision". Then, the voice said "Many people say, "yes" with their lips, but to understand and receive the fullness of God's love, you must say it with your heart every day." I felt overwhelmed and knelt down on my knees and I began to worship and praise God for loving me and for giving me another chance to live.

When I looked up, Rochelle was standing over me. She took me by the hand, and I followed her out of the room where she said "what you've done today was the most important decision a person could ever make in life. She led me to the room called "CHANGE". At this point, I was asking myself "Why?" I was feeling so good that I was ready to take on the world and begin this new life.

The room was full of people, and as I looked around the room, I saw a few of my friends sitting in the crowd. I found a seat right in front of Nyna and Wendell. Without saying anything, we made eye contact and smiled, and Wendell gave me a high-five. Nyna then leaned forward and whispered "God is Good". She had a huge smile on her face, and I could tell by the look in her eye she was feeling just as good as I. As I sat there waiting for the speaker to come out, I began to thank God for being in my life, and for giving another chance to get life right. For me, personally, it felt like a load had been lifted off of my shoulders. At the same time, I was thinking "What could top this? This was better than any high I had ever had." At this point, all I wanted to do was be a Christian and serve God.

A tall African-American man with a bald head made his way to the podium. He introduced himself as Marcus. He said he had spent three years in prison before he, as he phrased it, "Woke up and smelled the coffee" and accepted Christ into his life before he entered this building.

Marcus welcomed us to the family of faith and, then, talked about how much God loves us and how much courage it took to accept Christ into our life. Then he said "be careful and do not use this experience as a quick fix for what brought you here to this building. Too many addict-alcoholics leave the building because they don't believe it can get any better than this. Some make it never to use again but many don't. They end up cheating themselves because God has done so much more for them. With Christ in their lives they return back to drinking and using. They fall in love with the feeling of being saved, and having a made up mind to be a Christian, believing that this feeling will keep them free from their addiction. Remember God brought you here for a reason and recovery is more than staying free from drugs and alcohol." He then said "Only 5 percent of your problem was your addiction 95 percent is you and your thinking, your behavior."

Next, he started to talk about what was on the other side of the large doors on the 3rd floor. "I had plum forgotten about those doors". He told us that once we walk through the third floor doors, you will be introduced to God's character, personality, and nature.

Marcus continued on by saying "On this floor, God will paint a picture of Himself. Understanding who God is very important as you build your relationship with Him. Remember He is the God who knows everything. He is the beginning and the end, the first and the last. He knows what is going to happen before it happens. God knows your thoughts, and our motives behind all of our actions. God knows if we are here for a quick fix, or if you really want a change in your life."

All of a sudden it made perfect sense coming from a perfect God. Then, Marcus talked about the difference between God being "God in our lives" and God being "Lord over our lives." He said "God in our lives means we recognize the presence of God and the power of God. Sometimes we check-in with God and sometimes we do not. For those that only recognize the "God in your life" understand God's power, but they use God like a "Spiritual Santa Claus" calling on God only when they need Him. Even though "God is in your life", people like this think they are doing God a favor by showing up on Sunday morning.

The goal should be allowing God to be "Lord over your life" learning how to bow down before Him in awe- understanding that God is all-powerful and has our best interest at heart." Marcus told us not to worry; all we had to do was learn how to check in with God for everything. Those that allow God to be "Lord over their lives" will understand their place in God's kingdom and worship Him for who He is. Once you make him Lord, your relationship with God changes, and it is easy to surrender to His will for your life.

Marcus asked us to reach across the seats and grab each other's hands, and He began to pray thanking God for bringing us to this point in our lives. As he continued to pray, I felt tears of joy roll down my face. He, then, said, "Make their hearts a clean heart O Lord and renew a right sprit within them". He asked us "if we were ready to make a quality decision to let God have complete control over our will and lives? Without looking up, I said, "yes". When he finished, we were all given new t-shirts that read, "24/7 Christian."

Rochelle then led me back to the 3rd floor and back to the step that led to the massive doors. I started up the stairs towards the door past the life changing words that were engraved in the marble steps, which were now engraved in my soul. Alone, again, I went up a few more steps, "What does it mean to be a 24/7 Christian? Do I have to act a certain way? Will I have to change my personality? Will I be a Holy Roller? I really don't want to be a phony; I've been that too long. What if I fail as a Christian? What if I can't be a 24/7 Christian? All these things were going through my mind as I walked up the steps toward these magnificent doors. With every step I took, the doors slowly opened. With every step, a light came on inside my spirit.

As I approached the large beautiful doors, and to the right engraved on a gold plaque was a set of instructions that read "making it through this floor requires making an honest attempt to live right". When I reached the top of the steps, the doors opened up completely. As I walked through the doors of this room, suddenly I was standing at the top of a small hill that overlooked another valley. There were thousands of beautiful trees down in this valley. A large sign at the edge of the valley welcomed me and called this valley the "Hiding Place." Under the sign was a huge stone tablet that had letters engraved in it. A shoulder strap pouch or bag of some sort also hung off of the tablet. The tablet instructed me to take the pouch and with it I was to gather some of the fruit from the trees in this valley.

Next to that tablet was a map of some kind. On this map was a picture of each tree, each bush and everything else in this valley. First, I noticed the large field of flowers. These flowers stretched from one end of the valley to the other, blowing gently in the breeze. The inscription on the map called these flowers "peace be still."

There were other trees in this valley. Most of these trees resembled fruit trees. On these trees were different fruits. There were hundreds of small trees in the valley. These trees were called "trees of joy." There were also hundreds of large trees. They were called "trees of love." There were also bushes that stretched along the streams of water; these bushes were called "security." In the middle of this beautiful valley was the oldest tree in the valley and its branches reached to the heavens. This tree was called "long suffering."

Over on the east hill, there were different color trees. The green trees were called "kindness." The light blue trees were called "goodness." To the west there were yellow trees called "faithfulness," "gentleness," and "self-control." All of these trees were full of fruit more than anyone could ever imagine or consume. In every group of trees, there were two trees that stood amongst each group. These trees stood like soldiers that watched over each group. They're very presence overshadowed each group of trees. These trees were called the trees of "forgiveness."

I started walking down into the valley. I could hear the sound of rushing water. The sound came from a stream that ran along the bushes called "security." This stream branched off and fed all the trees in the valley. This stream was no ordinary stream. It almost looked alive as it darted in and out of the trees, flowers, and bushes. It was a powerful moving stream, yet, it was gentle enough to walk across. The stream seemed to feed each group of trees giving the trees life. I walked up to the stream, knelt down and cupped both hands to take a drink. The water was cool and refreshing, and I could feel the water flowing through my whole body. A sign near the edge of the stream said, "O taste and see that the Lord is good."

Enjoying every minute of this, I sat down amongst the flowers and trees. I felt hypnotized. I took out my Bible and read the story of the woman with the issue of blood who pressed through the crowd and said to herself, "*If I could just touch the hem of His garment*, I will be alright." As I continued to read the story, I wondered who told her to touch the hem of His garment. I thought to myself that this was a perfect example of faith. I made up my mind right then that I wanted that kind of faith. As I lay back in this soft green grass, I could not help but think how good God has been to me in that He gave me another chance at life.

I was surrounded by beautiful flowers, and the rays of sun filled the valley. The sunshine consumed my entire body. From the top of my head to the bottom of my feet, a warm sensation rushed through my body immediately filling what seem like a void inside. In times past, I always tried to fill this void inside of me with drugs, alcohol, wine, women, songs, money and power. However, now I had finally found the real thing that completely filled this void for the very first time. I had never before felt such a sensation in my life. Was it possible that I could feel this way forever? At that moment, my belief in God grew by leaps and bounds, and one would have to be crazy not to want to serve a God such as this.

I knew deep down in my heart that God was with me and that He had a special calling on my life, but what that calling was I had no clue. A light rain began to fall. The drops of rain felt like a cleansing, refreshing spray that washed all of my wrong doings away. I closed my eyes and thanked God for bringing me here to this wonderful place and point in my life.

When I opened my eyes, I felt like a new person. Minutes later the sun started to shine as I laid back soaking up the sun's rays. As the rays fell upon my face, I watched the trees and the beautiful flowers paint a priceless picture in this valley that had me mesmerized by its splendor. Only God could put something like this together, I thought. I had no idea what was next in this building, or in my life, but for some reason I knew if I stayed with God everything was going to be all right.

I took another drink of water from the stream and lay back down amongst flowers that were called "peace be still." Once again, I closed my eyes and I let this great feeling consume me. The smell of the flowers filled my nostrils as I slowly dozed off. Falling into a deep sleep, I began to dream about where I had come from, and about all that I had been through. In each incident, at the time, it looked like there was no way out. I was either rescued or had barely escaped. So, in hindsight, I see that God was with me all the time. "Why, God?" I asked myself. "Why couldn't I have found you a long time ago? Why did I have to go through all that hell, pain, shame, and heartache for years?" I wasn't quite sure of the answer, but I was sure that if I stayed around I was going to find out. In my sleep, I was strengthened with peace and joy. As I fell deeper into sleep, I dreamed about a better life serving God.

When I awoke, I looked towards the rolling hills, and a thick fog began to creep over the valley, consuming everything in its path. Over the mountains and down into the valley, the fog covered this low-lying area like a blanket. First, fear set in and, then, I thought, "Everything in this valley has been good to me so why should I fear?" The fog was about two stories high, and moved like a slow moving train that devours everything in its path. So with anticipation, I waited as I watched the fog inch closer. When it finally reached me, I closed my eyes as it consumed my whole body. I felt something enter my body and figured this must be the God's spirit. Suddenly something leap inside me as if it had found a long lost friend. It was almost as if something inside me knew it was coming and had been waiting for its arrival. I could barely control myself as I lay there enjoying every moment. My body lay still but my insides raced around as if my whole being was jumping for joy. I welcomed this feeling into my life, and on that day, I knew I was filled with God's precious Spirit. I arose and began to praise God for my life. I ran through the fog that was now lifting. I made my way through the field of flowers and along the stream thanking and praising God for giving me another chance at life.

What a feeling, it was hard to explain, I was higher than I had ever been on any illegal drug (and I had tried them all). I finally found what I had been looking for all my life. The void inside me that hungered for something was finally filled. All my teenage and adult life I have tried to fill that void with drugs, women, money, and whatever made me feel good. However, none of these things "fixed" me. They were all fake, imitation. I had finally found the real thing.

Hours went by and I was still praising and thanking God for giving me another chance and putting me on the right road that led to Him. I began to thank God for everything; I thanked Him for my family who locked me out of their lives because of my behavior. I thanked him for the police that arrested me and threw me in jail. I even praised God for allowing me to be a junkie and living the destructive life style. Was I losing my mind? No, on the contrary, I have finally found my mind. I think I understand now. I was so hard headed and so full of pride that the only way God could get my attention was for me to go through what I went through, falling flat on my face. However, this time, I fell right into God's arms.

Some people are introduced to God at a young age and they are smart enough to surrender to God when they are first introduced. I took the long way around, but I am so glad I made it. I thank God for giving me another chance, but why? "Why is God showing me so much love?" I was an enemy to God. I sold dope, I turned people on to dope and some are still hooked. Why was God showing me so much love in spite of my past?

Guilt began to consume me, so much so that I dropped to my knees and I asked God to forgive me for all that I had did and been. I ask Him to forgive me for turning people on to alcohol, drugs, and introducing some to this destructive lifestyle. All of a sudden, the guilt was on me so heavy that, in an instant, I had forgotten all about this beautiful valley. The tears of joy had now turned to tears of sorrow. I did my best to fight against the sadness that was now consuming me, but I was consumed by the fact that many people were addicted to drugs because of me. Wiping the tears from my eyes I looked up and noticed the trees and the fruit in this valley.

I walked over to the tree of "forgiveness". Could it work for me? I realized that the only way to find out about forgiveness was to step out on faith and see. With no more excuses, I walked over to the tree of forgiveness and grabbed the fruit off of the tree and took a bite. Thunder rang out in the valley. Clouds started to form in the sky, and the storm began to move towards me. The closer the storm got the more violent the lightening storm became. As the clouds came over the hills, thunder rang out again, and the clouds got bigger and darker as they joined together in the sky. As I stood there watching these large clouds come towards me, the clouds began to form some words in the sky. By the time it reached me, I could see that this big black cloud formation spelled out *PSALMS 103:12* and stopped directly over my head. As the cloud positioned itself directly over my head, I dropped to my knees and looked directly into the cloud and it started to rain. The rain began to fall all over me until I was drenched. It kept raining until the cloud turned completely white and there was no more rain left in the clouds. With my eyes closed, head tilted back and the water running off my face, the sun came out and filled the valley. Within seconds I was completely dry. When I stood up, it seemed as if a heavy load was washed away and I felt 30 pounds lighter.

My body was losing all strength as the sun filled the valley. My knees began to buckle, so I sat down before I fell down. The guilt was gone and, once again, I felt like a new person. God had entered my life, and I was willing to give God total control. I leaned back against the tree of "forgiveness" and looked across this magnificent valley that had truly changed my life when a rainbow appeared. Its colors stretched across the sky and landed on top of a hill not far from where I was sitting. Curiosity got the best of me, so I gathered my strength and began to walk towards the rainbow. However, before I left, I grabbed some more of the fruit from the tree called "forgiveness". As I got closer, I could see that the rainbow fell on one specific tree. From where I was standing, I could not tell what type of tree it was. When I reached the area where the rainbow had fallen, I had entered the "Trees of Self Control".

The way I had been living before I arrived in this building, it was certain that I had no idea what self-control was and knew I had none of it. On my own, I knew I did not possess the ability to stop using, so I asked myself, "What was the definition of self-control?" One thing that I had learned while in this building was not to question everything or try and figure everything out and to just do it. I grabbed what looked like an apple and took a bite. For a few moments, nothing happened. I took another bite, and the air got completely still as if I was suspended in time. Slowly the rainbow started changing colors one at a time. Faster and faster, the color range of the rainbow began to change in sequence like flashing lights on a Christmas tree. All of a sudden, the changing of colors stopped. The earth began to shake. The leaves on the tree of "self control" fell off of its branches straight to the ground and into the formation of an arrow.

The leaves pointed to a cave that had been shaken open by the earthquake. I started making my way over to the cave. I could not see inside from a distance because it was so dark. As I got closer, a strong wind came from inside and it hit me almost knocking me down. Leaning into this wind, a voice came from inside and said, "The key to self-control is having a made up mind to follow God's instructions. The wind ceased and everything was calm again. "What a simple message," I thought. At this point, I was willing to do whatever was suggested. I sat down at the edge of the cave, took my Bible out and looked up PSALMS 103:12. It read, "As far as the east is from the west I have forgotten your transgressions." Joy once again filled my body and I thanked God for not holding my old life over my head.

I stayed on this floor reading the Word of God, tasting, and gathering fruit from all the trees. I stored the fruit in my bag knowing I would need some fruit at a later time. I stayed in this room for at least a month, drinking from the stream, reading the Word of God, and restoring my soul. I have never felt so good in all of my life.

It was time to move on to the next floor and a powerful urge came upon me to leave this building again and continue on with my life. This was the strongest feeling yet. I felt I had received all that I needed to make it in life just from being here on this third floor. God has surely proven His Love for me, so why should I stay any longer? This time I was not buying it. I truly believed my own head was out to get me.

As I walked out of this room, two attendants immediately met me. One introduced himself as Big Don. He was like his name, a muscular guy that could have played on any ones football team, and a woman named Autumn. She was a tall, cute African American girl.

The look on their face was of panic. Before I could tell them about my wonderful experience on the third floor, Don began to tell me about the importance of finishing this process called recovery and the worst thing that I could ever do is leave at this point. Autumn then said "God did not bring you into this building and then change His mind; He brought you here for a reason...to finish the process". "Many people at this point are so overjoyed by the spirit inside them being renewed they forget there is another part of them that has to be renewed. Big Don jumped in and said "this is the fleshly man inside you, the one that liked to smoke dope, party, drink, and stay out all night. This fleshly man wars against the spirit man and draws you back to the old life style, under the umbrella of being saved." Without letting me get a word in edgewise, Autumn said, "many are deceive at this point and they leave the building convinced that God will keep them free from drugs and alcohol." It was evident that many people choose to leave the building at this place and time.

Clearly they were double teaming me and they wouldn't let me say anything. Autumn continued "to leave now would not be God's will for your life." Big

Don then said something that really caught my attention, "More people leave this process called "recovery" when things are going well rather than when things are going poorly. So be on guard; the enemy's job is to distract you and move you from where God wants you to be."

Knowing that I was not going anywhere, I continued listening to what they were saying as they led me to an area where the elevators were stationed. The intensity and passion in their voice let me know that this was a turning point for many. It was easy to see why. This new life that God reveals to us is mind-boggling, and it is easy to take your mind off our previous life and move forward in this new life. Once in this area, I noticed arrows pointing to a set of elevators. There was one big difference about these elevators. The arrows on the outside of the elevator door now indicated Up and Down when the previous elevators only went "Up". Autumn and Big Don was now giving me an option to continue on in this "process called recovery" or leave the building all together. I pushed the button to continue up and both Autumn and Big Don gave each other a high-five, shook my hand, and left.

When the doors opened, there was another shock. The entire elevator was made of glass. What was this all about? What was it they wanted me to see? I stepped into this glass elevator and the doors closed slowly behind me. On the previous floors, the elevators automatically moved to the next floor. Instead of moving, the elevator just sat there until I pushed the up or down button.

It was at this time I thought about some of my friends whom I met while here in this building. How were they doing, or were they still here, I wondered. As I pushed the button that was marked 4th floor, the elevator slowly started inching upward. I turned around and what I saw blew my mind. As I looked out of this glass elevator, as far as the eye could see, there were hundreds of elevators scattered out in this vast area. I had to pinch my leg just to remind myself again that I was in a 12-story building on the east side of town. In each elevator, there was a passenger inside gazing out into this vast area. The elevators that were going up were taking passengers to different floors in this huge open space. Stopping at each floor I could see a person exiting the elevator onto the floor. As I looked up through the top of this glass elevator, I could see some elevators going so high that they were going through the clouds. But that wasn't the biggest shock, there were elevators going down. These elevators didn't stop, they continued down to the bottom which looked like the basement.

Not far from me, about 25 feet away, an elevator slowly inched its way down. Inside this elevator there was a young man who sat on the floor of the elevator. He looked weary and confused. He looked right through me as he gazed out of the elevator. The elevator did not stop at any of the floors, it continued going straight down towards the basement. A sign on top of the elevator read "NOT WILLING TO CHANGE – NOT WILLING TO SURRENDER".

What a wakeup call, and hard to believe that some people were going back to the basement and starting over or leaving this building all together. As the elevator continued up, I knew that I could not go back down. I was willing to do whatever it took to stay clean and sober and make a successful attempt at this new life. I prayed to God immediately because I knew I was no different than that man that just left the building moments ago.

As the elevator inched up, a TV monitor located just above the door came on and a recorded message began to play. A very jovial woman dressed in bright colors was on the screen. Balloons and streamers were falling down behind her, and marching band played in the background. She then asked if I would like to take a break from the Recovery Process and go to a specially designed floor and have some clean fun.

As the marching band continued to play in the background and balloons and streamers fell from the ceiling, she said that it is possible that I would meet some of my friends in this room between the 3rd and 4th floor. This room was designed to relieve some of the pressure of everything you have learned while in this building. If so, push the yellow button that is flashing on the panel. Wow! Sounds like a party on this floor, can't hurt to check it out! I looked down at the flashing yellow button and pushed it. All of a sudden, the elevator came to a complete halt.

The doors opened, and I stepped out into a lobby where other elevator doors opened at the same time and out of those elevators people like myself stepped out. A group of us was greeted by a young lady with a big smile and she said, "Welcome to the room where time stands still. You are welcome to visit this room anytime while here in *Recovery Tower*. There is no time limit while on this floor, so relax and enjoy, and you may return to recovery at your leisure. Have fun and take it easy! There is only one condition", she then handed us a plastic card and said, "in order to participate in any activities on this floor, you must read what is on the card to the attendant that monitors each activity room". I looked down on the card and one side read, "The process of recovery is an ongoing process, Trust in God and continue." The other side read "Put off till Tomorrow Floor."

After reading the card, she gave us a brochure concerning all the activities available on this floor. On the front cover of the brochure was the words "Put off till Tomorrow Floor".

I thought that was an odd name for a floor, but thinking nothing of it I closed the brochure and moved on. While walking down the corridor, I opened the brochure and on the inside there was a long list of things to do. In one room, there were pool tables, game boards, big screen televisions and ping-pong tables. The next room was a very large room where people were jogging, exercising, and working out with all types of sports equipment. There were several large swimming pools, a bike-riding track that maneuvered its way throughout this large room. Through another door was a room where people were sitting at computers. Some were surfing the web, others were looking at job possibilities, while others were filling out employment applications. I was told some were accepting jobs and leaving *Recovery Tower* all together. There were reading rooms, music rooms, and computer rooms. People were extremely busy - buzzing around like bumble bees - as if they did not have a care in the world.

I had not checked my email since I arrived in *Recovery Tower*. I walked into the computer room to read my e-mail when I was stopped by an attendant who asked me if I had my card. "Oh, yea, I replied, as I reached into my pocket and pulled out the card. I read the wording, "The process of recovery is an on-going process. Trust in God and continue." The attendant, then, allowed me into the room.

After checking my e-mails, I involved myself with some of the activities on this floor. There was a golf course on this floor so I played a round of golf and I made some new friends. Some of them told me that they have been on this floor for weeks, even months.

After my second day in this room, I ran into a couple of the faithful 12, Annette and Rodney. It was so good to see some familiar faces. We found a quiet place and began to share about our third-floor experience. Everyone agreed that this experience was one that we would never forget. Rodney said he now understood the meaning of faith. Annette talked about the trees, the fruit, and the infilling of the Holy Spirit.

We talked about riding in those glass elevators and seeing how many people were involved in getting their lives together. We talked about the elevators going up through the clouds into a 12 story building on the east side. The tone changed when we started talking about those who were going down and the sign on top of those elevators that read, "NOT WILLING TO CHANGE – NOT WILLING TO SURRENDER". We all agreed and vowed to continue on no matter what. I think the most important and most exciting thing we talked about was accepting Christ into our lives.

It was then that we decided to look for the rest of our friends. In and out of every room, we searched. Some rooms were so large it took hours to examine the entire area. At the end of the day we decided to take time out and go to the room called "CHANGE", and it was there that we heard some very good sharing. Some of the hurdles people had faced are profound, and it is a miracle we are all still alive to talk about it.

A classy, refined well-dressed little lady approached the podium dressed in a business suit she said her name was Ndey. After looking at her you'd never know she was a black-out drinker. She shared a little bit about herself and then she began to talk about her visit to the floor called "Procrastination". She had 20 years of freedom from her addiction and said "it is real easy to get side-tracked while in recovery. Many of you under the sound of my voice will never reach your full potential or make it to the 12th floor. Recovering people have addictive personalities and we get addicted to things that have nothing to do with our personal growth or recovery! We are easily distracted by people places, and things. These things can be legal, safe and fun but have nothing to do with keeping you clean and sober. Never forget your primary purpose, "Recovery". Ndey then talked about some of her friends who took their eye off of the prize and then relapsed after five, ten, fifteen years of being free.

"Don't forget the reason you came into this building," she said. "You had a serious problem with drugs or alcohol or both. Staying clean and sober is first, and many of you have received much more.

Never forget one hit is too many and a thousand never enough! All it takes is one hit or drink and the hell you just left all comes back! Sometimes double or triple the pain."

Ndey then said "How many of you noticed elevators going back down towards the basement?" At that time everybody raised their hands. Then she said, "Some must die that others might live! In other words you have to learn from their misfortune".

"Kind of harsh" I thought but real. I was frightened by those that left Recovery too soon. Maybe they didn't take recovery seriously, may me they weren't real alcoholic/addicts. Ndey then said, Don't forget the pain that drug and alcohol took you through. And don't be impatient; it will take time to erase some wrongs in your life. It took years for you to mess your life up and it will take time restore it back to some type of normal lifestyle. Don't be like some that just hang around recovery, instead get involved with your recovery.

For some people, relapse becomes a motivator for those that have not taken recovery seriously. It is their misfortunes that will make others get serious about their recovery. Take the cotton out your ears and stick it in your mouth."

I leaned over to Rodney and said, "Home girl is hard!" He replied, yea, "it's tough, but it is fair." She continued by saying, "Doing meaningless things everyday gets old, and if you are not growing, you are regressing - going backwards". Ndey was hard, some of what she had to say to us was difficult to swallow, but she was real. You could hear a pin drop as she brought it "straight no chaser." She talked about first having a plan for recovery and then setting her goals. Eventually, she made up her mind to go back to school, and, now, she works on Wall Street as a stock broker. This was a dramatic difference from what she used to do.

When we walked out of that room, we all knew we had to make a decision; either stay here in this room and have fun, enjoying life for a while, or continue on and see what God had in store for us.

We decided to talk about it over donuts and coffee. While drinking coffee we saw one of our friends who are a part of the "Original Twelve." It was Janet, the single parent. We saw her horseback riding in one of the hobby rooms. When she saw us, she jumped off of her horse and ran to us. We all embraced and, once again, we began to share our experiences with her. I asked her if she had seen Shorty and, to my surprise, she had. We were all happy to hear that he was still participating in this recovery process. Janet told us that Shorty only stayed for a day and he continued onto the fourth floor.

That was all the confirmation we needed. We, too, decided to move on to the fourth floor, but, to our surprise, Janet was not ready to move on. Annette pleaded with her to continue on and to remember everything we learned on the previous floors. However, Janet told us she was having too much fun and that she had met a man on this floor whom she enjoyed being with. I reminded her of her responsibilities and about her children who were waiting for her on the outside of this building. Janet angrily said that she was not leaving the building, that she was not abandoning recovery, but that she was only taking her time as she had fun here in the "Put off till Tomorrow Floor". It seems like the name "Put off till Tomorrow Floor" had come to life in a real way. Janet had forgotten why she came into this building in the first place. It was a sad sight to see. Rodney reminded us about being powerless over people, places, and things, and that we could not make Janet or anybody else do anything. I think we were starting to understand more about this sickness called addiction and about the process of recovery.

For me, it was simple. There was more to life than having fun, and the only way I could do this was get all of the benefits out of this building while I was here. As Janet mounted her horse, we all looked at her as she read her card out loud. "The process of recovery is an on-going process. Trust in God and continue." We all looked at each other and then glanced back at her. As we left the room, she looked back at us, and I felt that she knew she was doing the wrong thing. We all pulled out our cards and threw them in the trash. The answer to what we had to do was written on each card. "The process of recovery is an on-going process, trust in God and continue".

I thought about Janet and others like her who seemed to be wasting valuable time because they are afraid to move on. Unfortunately, I could not talk about them because I thought about leaving and I am no better than them. All I could do is pray for Janet and move on.

When we made our way back to the elevators, we noticed our names were over each door. Rodney asked us all to promise that we would not get sidetracked, but continue on in this building until we reach the end. We all promised, and Annette suggested that we pray together before we left. She looked at me and asked me to pray. Before I could decline (which was what I wanted to do), everyone grabbed each other's hands and formed a circle. "Wow!" I thought, and my heart started beating a mile a minute. Again I felt like I was swimming in uncharted waters, praying out loud in front of people really made me feel uncomfortable. Everyone stood in silence with their heads down and eyes closed waiting for me to begin. I thought about the task at hand and I asked God to guide us, protect us, and teach us. I prayed for Janet and her family and that she would wake up and continue on in her recovery. I thanked God for being our Father and giving us another chance at life. I finished the prayer, and we all praised God together.

We all hugged each other and vowed to continue on. I looked back towards the room where Janet was at, hoping she would come around that corner with us, but she didn't.

All of our elevators opened at the same time, and we all entered. Once the elevator doors closed, a voice came over the intercom and said, "If you wish to continue, and you don't understand the tools you received on the 1st, 2nd and 3rd floors, you can return to the basement and start all over again. In order to make it through the rest of this building, you must apply what you learned on the first three floors daily. Remember, "God will never leave you or forsake you."

When the doors opened onto what I thought was the 4th floor, I noticed people reading what looked like an inscription on the wall. The inscription read:

ABOUT THE 4TH FLOOR

It will take courage.

God did not bring you this far to leave you – Walk like, act like, and talk like everything will be all right.

Prepare to take a trip back into your past (Fear Not, God Is with You.) On the 4th floor it is important you be honest, be thorough, and fearless.

Also remember these things:

• God loves you. Remember you are on a journey. You will begin at one point and God will guide you down a path of safety.

• Fear not, your past cannot hurt you.

After watching Janet trip, I was ready to move on to the 4th floor. At that moment, a muscular built man walked up to me and stuck his hand out and introduced himself as Leon. Leon stood about 6'6 and could have easily been a bodybuilder. Without letting my hand go, he asked me if I was serious about getting better. I told him "yes", He then said "are you ready to continue with this process? Again I said yes. He smiled, released my hand and gave me a card that said, "Sponsor." He told me that from here on until the 12th floor he would be Leon which meant he would be a "stone's throw away" to assist me whenever I needed it.

He then said "a sponsor is a person that has been through this process and now gives back as a part of their own personal growth. Someone was here for me when I walked through the doors of recovery and hopefully you will be here for someone when and if you complete this process." I thought about it but quickly my mind could not grasp helping anyone but myself!

He then said, "No man is an island unto himself," and going through this process you must learn to trust in people. He told me that anytime I needed help just take the sponsor card and slide it in the available slots on each floor. Many people try to make it through recovery thinking that they are wise enough to figure the program out. They seem to forget that they were doing their best thinking and they became addicted to drugs, alcohol or both.

Leon was too big to say "no" to because any other time I would have declined. I came from a neighborhood where you stand on your own two feet, and you don't ask for help. But what I have learned in this building, so far, my old ways got me here. So I put his card in my pocket, and he led me back to the elevators.

Uncover The Madness

Secrets Keep You Bound!

Fourth Floor

As the elevator took us up to the fourth floor, I boldly stood there waiting for the elevator doors to open. Once they opened, Leon again asked me if I willing to go to any length to become what God wanted me to be, and I replied, "yes". He said "the program will work if you work it."

He led me to what looked like a moving sidewalk. There on the moving sidewalk, was a reclining chair. The chair was facing towards what looked like a stage. As we walked up to the chair, I could see a button on the arm of the chair with the word "PRINT" beneath it. On the other arm, was a red button that read, "STOP" and beneath that button was a green button that read, "START." On the floor next to the chair was a box of tissue.

Leon said "here, on this floor your past will be presented to you in a real way. Some of the things you will see will be pleasing and some not so pleasing, but all these things made you who you are today. But fear not God was with you then and he is with you now. Take your time and every once in a while stop and examine your past closely. Answers to who you are and why you do what you do lie hidden in your past. Leon then pointed to a slot on the inside of the arm rest. Underneath the slot were instructions that read, "When in trouble or have questions, insert sponsor card". I reached in my pocket to make sure I had not lost the card before taking a seat. When I looked up, Leon was gone.

Before I got started I said a little prayer "God go with me". I leaned back in the chair and hit the "start" button. The escalator began to move sideways. As the moving sidewalk went around the first of many bends, it came to a stage and, to my surprise; a real live re-enactment of my life was being played out before my very eyes.

There I was, a young kid, growing up at my parents' house. Everyone was in the backyard, barbequing, playing cards, dominos, just having a good time. It was not uncommon to meet over my mother's house every Sunday to break bread. In this re-enactment, everyone in my family was there: my mother, father, two brothers and two sisters. It was here that I had my first shock on this floor. My oldest brother was killed in a car accident about four years ago, but there he was. I slowed the moving sidewalk up and took a good look at him. I still miss him to this day and the pain of him being gone was still present. Water filled my eyes as I reached down and retrieved some tissue.

My aunts, uncles, cousins, and friends were all in this re-enactment that made up my life. Even my dogs were there. Everyone looked so real. I yelled out to my Mom, but she could not hear me. I even whistled to my dogs, but they did not hear me either. The moving sidewalk began to slow up as it came to the high and low points of my childhood. This re-enactment showed my adolescent days: playing ball in the park, fishing, camping and just being a big brother to my brother and sisters. I had everything. The love of two parents giving me all the things I needed and some of the things I wanted. If we were poor, I didn't know it.

As the moving sidewalk traveled through my life the sidewalk paused at some periods longer than others. Taking chances, being disciplined for breaking rules and laws, seem to be common. Everything was not so smooth in my past and many things I had forgotten were tucked away deep down inside.

The sidewalk continued around one bend and slowed up coming to a complete stop. As everything began to unfold, it took a few minutes to figure out what part of my life was being played out. It was the first day of school where my brother and I were enrolling into a new elementary school. We had just moved into this neighborhood and our family was the only African American on our block.

The neighborhood we moved from was all black, so this was a big culture shock for all of us. I had never experienced racism, and had no clue what it was or that it even existed. From the very first day we entered this school, the kids let me know that I was black, something I didn't know from the school I came from. Because I was very dark in color even the few African American at the school joined in the tease. Every day I wanted to return to my former school but of course this was not possible. Kids teasing me because of the color of my skin affected me deep down in my soul. The next scene showed me at home locked in my bathroom crying and my mother heard me, she asked me what was wrong and I told her "I hated this new school and I also found out I hated being black."

As I sat in the chair watching my life being played out and seeing almost first hand all the hell I went through at this new school, I got angry all over again. Now, I understood where some of my anger came from and still to this day people try to label me as an "angry young black man." (Wonder Why?) Maybe there was some truth in it? No one told me how to deal with this type of hurt. I didn't have a concept of what racism was, and anger was my first line of defense. I also developed resentment towards my parents for enrolling me in a school and bringing me to a place where people hated me for the color of my skin.

The sidewalk moved slowly around another corner. I had a feeling it was going to be another shocker. Once again, it started off with my being at school and my teacher announcing to the class that my best friend had accidentally been killed. I had to be about ten years old when my best friend Freddie died. He was accidentally shot by his brother while playing with their father's gun. When I got the news at school, I ran all the way home and stayed in my bed for what seemed like a week.

Still to this day, I do not handle death well. The next scene moved to my friend's funeral. I am not sure what hurt me the most, seeing my friend laying there in the casket or hearing the cries of his mother sobbing uncontrollably. She was the kind of mother that picked us up from school and, sometimes, allowed me to eat dinner and sleep over. I hated seeing her in so much pain. I remember running up to her telling her that I would be her son. She held me so tightly, almost as if she was not going to let me go. I never wanted to let her go. As tears ran down my cheeks I reached over the chair and grabbed some more tissue to wipe the tears away.

Whether it was the pain of losing my best friend or being victimized by racism, it always seems to be something. The sidewalk continued passing through my life. From the bullies that terrorized me, to the pain and frustration of watching two parents arguing, separating, and ultimately divorcing, my life was filled with tragedy, drama, and chaos. This room was beginning to take its toll on me, so I hit the "stop button". I got out of the chair and took a walk around the room. I thought about calling Leon but decided not to. A thought came to my mind to take a break and go to the "Put off till Tomorrow Floor". "Wow!" I thought where did that come from?" I asked God to help me make it through and I returned to what I am now referring to as the "chair of pain."

I sat down and hit the "start button", and the sidewalk started moving through my life again. It traveled through the pains of trying to be accepted by people that may never accept me. Slowly it was being revealed to me that I was a "people pleaser." I wanted everybody to like me, and could not understand why some people didn't.

Memories of losing my brother, memories of failed relationships, memories of being in gangs, being shot going to so many funerals began to take its toll. Memories of being locked up in jail cells scared and alone, far away from my family and friends. What happens behind those bars I will never forget. All of these memories began to overwhelm me.

The escalator begins to slow down and the slot on the desk in front of me began to make a beeping sound. The word "sponsor" lit up and began flashing. At this time, I had an option to stop and call Leon if I wanted to or continue on. I decided to continue on. I just wanted to get through this nightmare called "my past". Later on, I would find out that this was one of my problems never trusting in anyone and never asking for help.

As the sidewalk started venturing through my adolescent life again, "as if it missed something the first time", I braced myself because I was sure they wanted me to see something in here that I overlooked initially. This time, the escalator stopped at the park where I played little league baseball. It also stopped at the school plays where I auditioned and was awarded for my acting. It took me back to when I used to sing in the school choir and every once in a while they would let me sing a solo. All of these things were good, but as I looked in the audience, no one from my family was there to share with me. At the end of each event, kids would run up to their mothers and fathers and celebrate their achievements, and I would leave and walk home alone. My father would always promise to come, but he never showed up. So there was no one there at none of my events, no one there to see me hit the home run, act out my lines, or sing the perfect note. All these things began to play out before me and immediately the emptiness inside my gut finally hit me like a ton of bricks. I hit the pause button and, once again, I felt so alone and just like back then, I believed no one cared. I closed my eyes in silence and asked God to help me make it again. After a few minutes, I lifted my head and saw the "Sponsor" light flashing again, so I thought about asking for help; however, I decided not to.

I pushed the "go" button, and the escalator moved to scene where my aunt walked up and looked directly at me while sitting in this chair and said, "Your daddy wasn't nothing, and you're not going to be nothing, you were born to be a failure and nobody cares about you. You're the worst thing that ever happened to my sister. All you brought to her was worry, pain and disappointment. Sometimes I wish she never would have had you!" and she walked off stage.

I hit the "stop" button, and the sidewalk came to a halt. That was it; I couldn't take it anymore. It was either talk to someone or take a drink! I pulled out the "sponsor card" and slid it into the slot. Leon appeared and told me to follow him. We walked down some stairs and through another set of doors and we were back on the third floor. We sat down in the tall green grass amongst the lilies and the flowers near the gentle stream. He then said "What took you so long to ask for help?" With my head down I said "I don't know I thought I could make it" He then said "remember your best thinking got you here, in this process called recovery you have to learn how to follow directions and trust in God as He works through other people. You can't do this by yourself"

Leon then said "you are not alone; the God that you met on this third floor is with you. God ordered our footsteps and arranged your life in such a way that He works through people and we have to trust Him." I told Leon that I had just been faced with things that I tried to forget for years. Things like losing my friend, my brother, and being hurt by evil people surfaced on this 4th floor. For about forty-five minutes, we sat there and Leon just listened to me. Just being able to talk about some of my hurtful past experiences seemed to be therapeutic because most of these experiences had been tucked away for so long.

Leon then reminded me of some of the dangerous situations that I had gotten myself into while drinking and using and it was a miracle that I was alive. "Even when you did not know God, He was taking care of you. It's not an accident that you are here in recovery at this time." He then reminded me of some of the things that I had been introduced to on the first floor like "acceptance." "Accept your past! He said and remember the good thing about the past, is that it has passed, it can't hurt you anymore.

He talked about "Faith" and what I learned on the second floor. Every time I took a step, the light came on and this was an outward sign of how much courage I received with every step. So I had to continue on believing everything was going to be all right. Then, he talked about what I had learned on this floor, the third floor. I looked around at the beautiful trees and the fruit that gave me strength.

At this time, a plate was brought to me on a beautiful gold-leaf platter. Atop this platter, nestled in the flowers called "security," was fruit I had seen and tasted on this floor. There were slices of joy, slices of love, and a few slices of faithfulness. I was given a large glass of water from the stream that protected the trees and gave strength to everything in this beautiful valley which was on the third floor.

Leon then led me to the room called "CHANGE." As I looked around the room, I noticed one of the "Faithful 12"; it was Dennis the truck driver. I found a seat next to him and turned my attention to the speaker when Dennis leaned over and asked me what floor was I on? I told him that I was on the 4th floor, and he said, he was also. He told me that he was having a very hard time dealing with his past. He said the only thing that was keeping him from leaving *Recovery Tower* was a sign he read when he first entered the building and that was, "one day at a time". At this point, he had it broken down to one hour at a time or even one minute at a time.

As the meeting began, a young stocky clean cut man named John was facilitating the meeting. John looked like a player at one time, and still may be. John wore a grey Brooks Brothers suit and a pair of penny loafers, but he also had a diamond earring in his right ear. To listen to John's story, he was an alcoholic in the worst way, a black-out drinker, but to look at him today you would not be able to tell that he ever took a drink at all. When he finished, he introduced a special guest to the podium to share.

A very beautiful Spanish girl made her way to the podium and identified herself as Lanita. She talked about being sexually assaulted by a family member as a child and her life spiraled out of control since then. With a smile on her face she said "My parents died before I knew them, I've been shuffled around from relative to relative never feeling truly welcomed by anyone, so I had deep abandonment issues. At the age of 14 I ran away from home and took care of myself. I became a prostitute at the age of 15, and continued to practice that lifestyle until I walked into *Recovery Tower* at 26 years old. I can't count how many times I woke up from a drunken blackout with no clothes on knowing that I had been sexually assaulted and abused." I've been in jail so many times it was like my second home.

I've heard some stories since I arrived here in *Recovery Tower* but what was different about this story was the freedom in which she told it. There was no shame, no guilt, and we could see God all over her. She had something that could not be bought, and that something was freedom. Lanita was free from her past and nothing in her past held her captive. She was able to move freely through life without being weighed down by what happened to her. She was so happy about being free that she began to praise God right in the midst of the meeting. We were so caught up in Lanita's joyful praise that we joined in with her, giving God all the glory and honor. What Lanita had was contagious, and I wanted what she had. I want to be okay in my own skin, I wanted to be free. When Lanita concluded, no one felt less of her because of what she shared.

John returned to the podium and asked, "If you want to be free, raise your hand and keep it up." Just about every hand went up in the room. "Okay lower your hands" Then he said, "In order for you to be free, you will have to uncover those secrets and one day reveal those secrets to another human being. Things that you said you would never tell anyone. In other words you will have to get butt naked honest! Secrets are the "elephants in the rooms" that can come back to haunt you when you least expect it. It can send you into depression; you can return to old habits and not know why it's happening. There are many ways in which we tried to block out our past, but we never forget them.

Because of what we've been through some people's behavior changes, *their angry, mean and bitter, and they don't know why, others are just unhappy and they never feel free because they spend most of their lives protecting their past. Others drink or use drugs or they live a wild and crazy life avoiding issues that might lead them back to their past.

Around every corner of your life there is a "trigger", something that will take you right back to your past. Some "triggers" are unknown to you; out of nowhere someone or something takes you back to a terrible time in your life. That's why here at Step 4th floor you confront your past. Here at Step 4 you learn to take the power out of your past a live free from it.

It takes courage to face your past and even more courage to share it with another human being. "So again I ask the question how many want to be free." After a long pause, one man raised his hand but to everyone's surprise he made his way toward the podium. He took a deep breath, put his hands in his pockets, and said, "Hi my name is Jim". After another long pause, he said "the reason I am here in "Recovery" was because of my drinking. My drinking really became a problem five years ago after being released from prison. I went to prison because I wrote some bad checks as a result of my gambling addiction. Gambling has always been my first love". He paused and put his head down. We could clearly see he was struggling. With his eyes towards the floor, his voice began to crack; we waited as he gathered himself. "I want to be free just like the lady that just finished sharing. There is no easy way to say this, so here it is. While in prison I was raped by two inmates and since that time I have not been able to come to grips with what happened to me. I have been drinking out of control ever since, I have thought about suicide but I'm too much of a coward, so all I do is drink". Quickly his sponsor joined him at the podium and put his arms around him and led him out the door that led to the valley called the "Hiding Place" on the 3rd floor.

Another guy made his way to the podium. He said "my name is Michael. I've been a Christian for most of my life but was introduced to alcohol at the age of 12. I grew up in a part of the country where my dad taught us to hunt and fish at an early age. I was about 17 years old when my buddies and I were hanging out in the woods drinking ,getting high and shooting at rabbits and cans, something that we did all the time.

On this day we spotted a guy walking along the railroad tracks. We jokingly started taking shots at him seeing who could get the closest without hitting him, but I accidentally hit the guy and killed him. We made a vow to never tell anyone, but for years, and to this day, it haunts me. No matter how much I asked God to forgive me, my head will not let me believe that I have been forgiven." Tears running down his eyes He returned to his seat where his sponsor hugged him. They, too, left and went to the valley called the "Hiding Place" on the 3rd floor.

My God, I thought, every story seems to get deeper and deeper and it is becoming clear to me why I have to face my past. If you do not face your past, it has a way of coming back to haunt you. For some reason, I thought if I did not think about those things in my past, they would just go away. So I started wondering how many problems, situations, and events I had actually hidden inside my soul causing them to lie dormant consequently causing me to suffer. How many secrets were actually keeping me bound?

Leon leaned over and said, "Your secrets do not have to be as deep and grim as what you just heard today, but secrets compounded on top of each other can be too much for any man or woman to carry. When we continue to stuff things that has happened to us in our past, our bodies are affected mentally and physically. The human body in this instance acts like a pressure cooker and if those negative things, toxins are not released in a controlled and safe environment, the individual ends up exploding. Some of us explode by drinking and using, others explode by gambling, overeating, or multiple relationships. No matter how you try to lead your life in a different direction, be it education, relationships, or successful professions, you cannot run from yourself! The best way to release this dangerous pressure is to face your past, accept your past and with God's help and recovery learn to let go of your past.

I put my head in the palms of my hands and started calling on God at that moment, I knew at this point I couldn't make it without Him. I appreciate this new relationship with God knowing that there was no human power that could save me from myself. I turned to Leon and asked him, "Is it possible to go through recovery without God? He said to me, "Yes you can, but those who make it through, live a bitter, angry, and empty life always leaning to their own understanding. It's called "crap-shoot" living. At the end of the day the void where God lives is never filled. Inside every man, there is a place where God lives and that void can only be filled by the Spirit of God."

On my way back to the fourth floor, I now understood why it was suggested that I take my time on the 1st, 2nd, and 3rd floors as it was crucial that I understand, grasp, and learn to apply all the tools that are introduced to me on those floors. Without powerlessness, acceptance, willingness, honesty, and faith, I would never have enough courage, to make it through the 4th floor.

I made my way back to the 4th floor and took a deep breath. I asked God to give me strength to make it through. I hit the "Go" button and continued back into my past. We finally left my adolescent period and moved to the next stage of my life which was the relationship phase.

The first person they show was my first love Gail in this re-enactment of my past. I had girl friends before her but Gail was my first love. The only problem with this relationship, I loved her more than she loved me. She was 18 years old and I was 19. I went "all-in" on this relationship never thinking she would cheat on me with a so-called friend. I still have a problem with him to this day. After my heart was broken by Gail I really hardened my heart with other women. It seem like I wanted to hurt them before they hurt me. I knew I was wrong because I had sisters that I protected from guys just like me but still I had a hard time trusting women. In my past I hurt a lot of women, lying to them and breaking their hearts. Today I see myself as a monster.

I dropped out of college in my 3rd year, things just weren't moving fast enough. I started selling marijuana and hanging out with the wrong crowd. The first time I went to jail another so called friend gave me up to knock some time off his case. My family spent a lot of money to keep me from going to prison. The second time I got busted I spent some time in the county jail for sales. Deep down inside me I knew I wasn't made for this type of lifestyle. After getting out of jail I drank and used even more.

Sitting in this chair on and off for 2 days watching my life being played back before me was difficult to say the least. Dreams destroyed, making wrong decisions, depression, oppression, and racism, no wonder I drank!

Going through my past also brought up all kinds of resentments and I blamed a lot of people in my past. The pain of seeing these things was as if it happened yesterday. As I sat there and compiled a long list of resentments, it was easy to see why I was always so angry. Resentments against people that I trusted in, family members, so called friends really played a big part of what I remembered. I was surprised that these resentments still affected me to this day. After all these years, I still thought of revenge.

As the sidewalk came around one of the final bends, I was so happy to see the end coming. I was truly tired of this part of the process called recovery. I wished I could run and hide, but where could I go and what would I do when I got there? I then remember a saying my grandmother used to say "everywhere you go there, you are". Never made much sense to me then but made a lot of sense now. As I slumped down in my chair, it felt great to end this roller-coaster ride through my life. Thinking that this nightmare was all over, I saw the "PRINT" button on the desk light up and it started flashing off and on. I took the sponsor card and slid it into the slot. Once again, Leon showed up and he hit the "Print" button and papers started coming out the side of the desk into a basket. It was a printed version of my entire life on paper. Leon gathered all the pages of my life, turned, and walked towards the door.

Suddenly, it seemed as if I was having an anxiety attack. My heart began to beat a million beats a minute. This was too much. First witnessing my whole life played out before me, bringing back things that I had purposefully hidden in the back of my mind because I truly wanted not to remember them anymore. Now, this stranger picks up the pages of my whole life and just casually walks away. This is too much. What was he going to do with them? There were unsolved crimes on those sheets of paper and if they fell into the wrong hands, I would surely serve some time behind bars. Where was he going with my secrets? Secrets I had kept to myself for years. Some I promised I would take to the grave.

Leon walked out of the room, down a long hallway, running behind him; he walked up to the elevator with my name on it. The doors opened, and he got on. As I stood there, I could not let this man out of my sight with my life in his hands. So before the doors could close, I ran to the elevator and jumped in. My heart was still racing. My eyes were fixed on those sheets of paper that all of a sudden became everything to me.

5th Step

You May Not Dance With Me, But You've Got To Dance With Somebody!

Dump It, Get Rid Of It, Let it Go!

Fifth Floor

The doors opened onto the 5th floor and Leon walked out of the elevator. Still saying nothing, he walked down a ramp that led to a small boat on a lake. He stepped down into the boat and sat down. Without hesitating, I followed him right onto the boat. There was no way I was letting him get away from me with my entire life story in his hands. My deepest, darkest secrets and some unsolved crimes were tucked under his arms. He stared straight ahead as if he were alone and said nothing, so I said nothing, but I never took my eyes off of him and those sheets of paper that was tucked under his arms. As long as they were in sight, I was all right.

At this time, I hardly noticed the boat had slowly moved away from the dock and was now drifting out into the middle of this large gentle lake. Finally I looked up and noticed the rolling hills that stood guard around this lake, they were erected like soldiers standing at attention, protecting all inhabitants that dwelled inside this peaceful setting. In the cliffs of these hills were several waterfalls that looked like sheets of glass that crashed into the lake silently.

Above us birds soared through the air, gently riding the breeze gracefully like ballerinas entertaining all who watched. Still my main focus was my life that was tucked under Leon's arms that, by the way, acted as if I was not even there.

The boat slowly moved toward the middle of the lake. Leon leaned over and handed me all the pages of my life. What seemed to be hours on this lake probably in all actuality was only just a few minutes as I had lost all sense of time as my life was literally in Leon's hands. Relief came over me as I held on to those pages as though my life depended on them.

Leon then lean back and began to enjoy the beauty that surrounded us. The waterfall, the trees, the birds, and how gentle and calm the water was. As I looked around this large lake, I noticed that there were other boats on the water. In each boat, there were two people floating around aimlessly. These boats had no engines, but there was a power that was not visible that slowly moved each boat around the lake. Each boat seems as if it had a mind of its own, going nowhere, but each boat had its own distinct destiny. On the side of each boat were the words "Let Go, and Let God."

One boat came within 50 yards of us. The vessel had just pulled away from the dock. The person inside the boat was Carmen. She was arguing and in a tug-of-war with her sponsor. Carmen grabbed hold of her "life on paper" and refused to let go. We slowly drifted apart and within minutes I could not see Carmen's boat anymore. Carmen always had a problem with this whole process, but I unfortunately could not concern myself with Carmen right now, I had to worry about what was going on with me. I turned my attention to my sponsor who was still enjoying this lovely lake and its surroundings. He was now leaning back with a big smile on his face. One hand was barely in the water making a wave as the boat moved through the water. He took a deep breath as if it were his last as he gazed into the horizon when it hit me again. I was in a 12-story building on 74th Street in the heart of the ghetto. Did I walk out a door somewhere and end up on another planet? If I was not sober, I would have sworn that I was high on something.

I guess Leon was finished taking his mental nap and said "The 4th floor is more than just digging up your past. There are situations and circumstances in every person's past that help define who they are. People that endure the 4th floor with their eyes, heart, and mind wide open recognize that God has been with them their entire lives. Through the ups and the downs, the good and the bad, those that move to the next level see God's hand.

Those that grab hold to this truth learn how to live their lives with humility and meekness as they learn to walk with God and appreciate God's awesome power. They are blessed to tap into this "spirit-building truth" early in their recovery, hurdling obstacles that might stifle others while leaving others dumb-founded. Those that do not see this truth struggle with change and unknowingly fight against God's plans for their lives.

Instead of surrendering to the mighty power of God, they try and fix their old lives, doing their best to put a square peg into a round hole. Frustration eventually gets the best of them, and they either leave recovery all together or they struggle through a clean and sober life, never experiencing the peace they could enjoy.

They may not be drinking and using, but they are experiencing the same drama, the same disappointments, and the same displeasure they experienced before addiction began. They have forgotten that they were doing their best thinking and they ended up addicted to drugs or alcohol. So they bounce off the walls of recovery never tapping into the peace that is ever so close if they would just choose this new life that could be theirs if they only surrender to the this process call recovery".

He blew me away when he started talking about God's awesome power and how God knew, when, where and what would cause us to surrender. God knew the day we would be born into this world and the day we would take our last hit, fix, or drink. "He has counted the hairs on our heads and knows everything about you." Leon talked about the different roads that people take in life and no matter how bumpy they may be, they all lead to God should we choose them with the free will God has given us.

Then he said "It is unfortunate that many of us come to God because of problems that occur in our lives, and we need God because we are facing impossible situations. What most people have a hard time grasping is God allows things to happen in our life because he knows these things will get our attention. "You exhausted every avenue to stop drinking and using before you surrendered right?" and I said "yes" For years I tried to stop on my own" And Leon said "that was the problem you tried to stop using your power and God will not get in the way of our self will.

We have to come to a point of total surrender. Once we reach that point in our lives, the miracle begins to happen for us."

Everything he said pretty much pertained to my life. Many people tried to tell me about God, but I was too busy to hear. The only reason I came to God at this point because I had run out of ways to change my life.

Leon then said "I was homeless at 8 years old, never knew my parents and I have no living relatives that I know of. Before I met God in this process of recovery 5 years ago I spent more years in jail than on the street."

"Wow!" My life was nothing compared to his and I had a tough life. I sat there in shock, as he shared the demoralizing things he did just to stay alive.

As I continued to listen, I recognized that the pain we went through was all the same. The names, places, and situations were different, but still the same shared pain. He then said "freedom and peace are found daily in this process called recovery. And to obtain this freedom and peace, all I have to do is recognize that God is ordering my steps. Today you have to learn how to let go of all of these secrets that have been holding you back". Leon told me to accept the past, because it was a part of my life, but to remember that it was the past, and it could not harm me now in the present. He told me to turn it over to God, because I've been carrying this load to long.

I told him that this was easier said than done. My past made me who I am today; the good, the bad, the ugly, and I have lived with these hurts and pain's my entire life. Then he replied, "It takes courage and faith to get better. Faith to believe that everything is going to be all right, and courage to let go and start anew everyday!

Once I realized I had nothing to lose but self-destruction, I asked Leon "what's the next step" He smiled and said "start reading the pages out loud". Shocked I paused, let out a big sigh and began to read. As the boat drifted aimlessly around the lake many times fear tried to consume me but I kept pressing on sharing things that I had told myself I would never reveal to anyone.

For at least an hour, I pressed my way through what sounded like a horror story, pausing for only a minute to take a break because the pain was so great. The whole time I was reading I dare not look up always wondering what Leon thought of me.

As I got to the end of my story, I buried my head in my papers. Once again, I felt low enough to play handball up against a curb.

Slowly the boat started heading towards one of the waterfalls. The water flowing off this particular fall was about 20 feet high. The sound of the waterfall splashing into the lake got louder and the mist filled the air the closer we got.

The front of the boat made a beeline straight for the waterfall, which by now had me hypnotized. As we got closer to the waterfall, Leon said nothing so I said nothing. The roar of the water crashing into the lake was electrifying. Slowly, the boat inched its way into the waterfall. As we went through the waterfall, I felt refreshed as the water covered my body. This water had to be from the streams that protected the trees on the third floor. From head to toe, I felt like a new person.

After going through the waterfall, we entered a small cave that took us to another lake that was just as large. There were boats on this lake with passengers on each boat obviously going through what I had just gone through. The boat slowly drifted towards a large waterfall that emptied out into a large body of water below. This waterfall looked like it was 30 to 40 stories high. The sound of the waterfall splashing into the lake below sounded like a fast-moving train rolling through town at top speed. I could see the mist making its way back up the falls as the boat inched closer to the edge. Before I could say anything, Leon told me not to worry as the boat got closer. In a calm voice, he said, "How can a person have faith in God and worry at the same time?" For some reason, this made a lot of since to me. The boat began to stop right at the edge just before going over the waterfall.

Leon then held out his hand nodding for me to give him my life on paper. I released the papers to him. He, in turn, gave me half of the papers back. Leon took his half and began to rip the pages into very small pieces. He told me to do the same. He then threw his half in the air and beckoned for me to give them to God. At this time, I threw them into the air, and they landed in the water. The force of the water circulated each piece around the boat and over the falls causing each piece of paper to disappear into the sea below. Leon told me that because many of the things that had happened to me are etched in my mind, a lot of what I experienced has been unforgettable. The key is not so much to forget, but to never let my past hinder or haunt my future.

GOOD!

As I watched each piece fall into the sea below, a sense of closure fell upon me. I saw a sign on the shore that read "The Sea of Forgetfulness." Slowly the boat turned around and headed back toward the other side of the lake. An overwhelming sense of peace enveloped me and a weight seemed to be lifted immediately off my shoulders.

I closed my eyes and began to thank God once again for His goodness and for this new life He so graciously gave me. For the first time in my life, I believed deep down in my soul that I had a chance of being free. Once out of the boat, I made a beeline to the room called "CHANGE." I also went to the 3rd floor and spent some time thanking, praising and enjoying God. I was able to read, study, and just take in all that I had learned since entering this building.

Along with others, I stayed on the 3rd floor for a week. I also spent some of this time in the room called "CHANGE." More and more, I could see that this room was going to be a big part of my life for the rest of my life. In the room called "CHANGE", I slowly began to open up and talk about my past. Here, I felt safe from mean people that did not understand what I was going through. I felt they understood because those in these rooms were just like me and would not judge me and I not them. We all have one thing in common; we are all people with a sickness who desire to be well.

On this day, I was leaving the room called "CHANGE" when I ran into Annette and her sponsor. Her eyes were red, and she looked like she had been crying. I gave her a big hug and she held me as if she never wanted to let go. She told me that she had just left the 4th floor, which was no joke. I did not know what was going on, but I could feel her pain. She found a seat as I sat near her.

When I felt it was time to move on to the next floor, I took my card and summoned my sponsor. We talked for a while, and then he led me to the elevators that would take me to the 6th floor.

Once on the elevator, Leon continued talking about this process called recovery, and how it was a lifetime commitment. He praised me for allowing God to work in my life and allow God to change me. He also told me that this journey was far from over. He told me that God was not finished showing me – Me – the new and improved me!

While standing in the glass elevator, Leon for some reason did not push the button to go to the next floor. We just stood there looking out into this vast space. I could see that there were fewer elevators going to the top and a lot more were going back down to the basement. "As the road gets longer, the people get fewer," he said. Then he shared with me that even though we threw my past sins into the "sea of forgetfulness" to rehash these things over and over can be just as detrimental as if we were still practicing them.

He talked about character defects that are born out of a dysfunctional lifestyle. These character defects are defence mechanisms that we use to protect ourselves while in our other lifestyles. Most of us do not realize we have them until they are pointed out to us. He then said, "Self will not reveal itself to self." Many of us live in denial about the character defects we have because we have a hard time facing the truth. First, these character flaws have to be recognized and labelled. After you can call them by name, you have to make a decision as to how you are going to reverse the behavior. That is, if you really want to eliminate them from your life. Some of these characteristics have been with us for so long; they have become an innate part of our personality. Leon turned and pushed the button to go to the 6th floor.

When You Look In The Mirror Who Do You See?

Don't Be Scared

Sixth Floor

The doors opened, and I stepped out of the elevator. When I turned to see what was taking Leon so long the doors slowly closed. He said, "Call me if you need me," and I could barely see his face as he waved goodbye. It was good having someone there who understood recovery and was available to help in a time of need. Without a sponsor, I doubt if I'd make it.

So what's next? Could anything be tougher than those last two floors? I made my way down the hallway, which led me to a strange looking door. It was dark gray in color with no doorknob. There was an "on" switch just above the light switch on the wall. I hit the switch, and the door made a funny sound as it began to come alive, to my surprise the door became a huge flat screen TV. I stepped back to get a better view of what was going on.

A cartoon character in the form of a banana appeared on the screen. This banana had arms, legs, eyes, a nose, and mouth. The banana began to speak, Welcome to the 6th floor and my name is "Humility." Here on this floor you will be faced with the behaviors, and character defects that were birthed from your dysfunctional lifestyle revealed on the 4th & 5th floor. Humility, then said, "To go high in God, you must be stripped of all unnecessary baggage and loads you continue to carry that stunts your growth." Then, this animated banana began to peal layers of its skin off its body until the skin was completely gone. The banana began to rumble and shake as smoke came out of the bottom of the cartoon character before taking off like a rocket disappearing from the screen.

The door finally opened, and what I saw looked very familiar. I walked into the room, and the door closed behind me. Not again I thought. I was back in my apartment, the apartment that changed my life on the 1st floor in the Honesty and Acceptance room. I hope I wasn't about to go through that again. I walked over to the window and I could see that this was more than my apartment, this was the whole neighborhood. The apartment across the street, people's homes on the block, and the gas station on the corner was all there. Even my car was parked on the street as people walked up and down the street.

Cars were moving down the street, and kids were playing on the block. This 6th floor seems like a real live version of my life just a few years back.

I turned back towards the door. There was a screen on this side of the door. The screen lit up and in the distance something was moving very fast towards the front of the screen and behind it was a trail of smoke. As it got closer, I could see a team of white horses pulling a chariot at top speed. Once the chariot arrived at the front of the screen, a little old man dressed up in Roman gladiator uniform with a big "T" on his chest introduced himself as "Teachable". He pulled out a scroll and began to read, "Hear ye! Hear ye! Frank you have just entered Reality World! For the next few days or however long it takes for you to understand this very important part of the process of recovery, you will live, work, and play. Here you will see just what kind of person you've become. Ha! Ha! Ha! Ha! Some things you will agree with and some things you won't. You will be exposed to parts of your life that make you who you are. Your character, personality, and temperament will all be exposed. It will be up to you to distinguish between what is good and what is bad, what is right and what is wrong.

The faster you learn, the faster you grow." The little gladiator boarded his chariot, and the team of horses rode off into the sunset. I walked into the bedroom and sat down on the bed. The alarm clock next to the bed began to ring. I picked up the clock and saw that it was 7:30am. The closet door lit up and the little Roman man named "Teachable" rode up again and said, "You have one hour to get down to your old job at the social services office". There you will begin your day in Reality Word!" He turned the steed of horses around and said, "Don't be late," and he took off again.

After college I took a job as a clerk at a Social Services Office. It was a good job but it really got in the way of my drinking and using.

I really didn't feel like working today. I had been through so much on the 4th and 5th floor. I just needed a day of rest. I decided that I would just call in sick today and show up tomorrow. So I walked over to the dresser and picked up the phone and called my supervisor. I told him I wasn't feeling well and that I would see him tomorrow. When I turned around, to my surprise, there was a large mirror hovering about two feet off the ground directly in front of my face. It was about 5 feet tall and 2 feet wide. I stood there stunned looking at myself trying to figure out what was going on with this mirror. At the bottom of the mirror, the words "Liar - Liar - Liar" began to scroll across the mirror. As I took a couple of steps toward the mirror, it moved two steps back. When I stopped, it stopped. It was the weirdest thing. Wherever I went, the mirror mimicked me staying about arms length away.

I walked back into the living room and the front door lit up again. Sitting behind a large desk in the middle of what looked like a football stadium was another cartoon character that introduced himself as "Truth." Truth stood up and I could see that he was dressed like a judge in a long black robe. Then another cartoon character flew into view. He looked like some sort of super hero. When he landed, I saw that he had a green cape, a green mask, and a white "W" on his chest. He introduced himself as "Willingness." "Truth" began to speak saying that they were there to explain what was going on, on this floor.

"Truth" began by saying, "Every time one of your character defects is being practiced by you; a mirror will show up to let you know which behavior is being practiced. That mirror will stay with you for five to ten minutes. This will give you time to become mindful of the defect and also give you time to think about the motive and why it appeared. "Willingness" jumped in and said, "Not everyone accepts these mirrors when they appear. Some people live in denial and are not willing to take a good look at themselves or change when they see it. "Truth" said that each mirror will identify itself by a scroll at the bottom of the mirror so that there will be no difficulty in identifying your problem." The screen on the door went blank, and when I turned around, the mirror was still there. At the bottom, the words LIAR – LIAR – LIAR scrolled across. I should not have told that lie about being sick for work. Slowly but surely, the mirror began to fade away until it was gone.

The door lit up again and "Truth" and "Willingness" were still standing there. Truth said "Your task is to examine the mirror and what caused it to show up. Willingness said "Then what are you going to do to correct your behavior?" Then "Truth" and "Willingness" turned and looked towards the sky. In the background, I could hear a rumbling sound. In the air, I could see the flying banana called "Humility" coming into view, and on the ground I could see "Teachable" on his chariot bolting towards the front of the screen. Once they all arrived, I now had "Willingness," Teachable," "Truth," and "Humility" standing in front of me.

"Teachable" began to speak. He said, "In order for you to grow and be successful on this floor, you will need to incorporate all of us into your life. During this time, if you are willing, you will learn some very valuable lessons."

Then Truth said, "You will need all of us in order to grow and become what God has called for you to be. Remember, this is only if you want a better life than the one you had.

"Humility" said, "Do not get frustrated as you start seeing the real you. No one is able to master this change overnight as this process takes a lifetime of work. The key to mastering this floor will be found in surrendering to what is right. Once your character flaws are revealed to you, you cannot deny them, instead acknowledge them and begin to work on correcting those areas that you now see. Some mirrors are bigger than others, representing the impact of a particular defect on your life and your personality. This directly affects you, and indirectly affects others around you. Of course, some mirrors will have more reoccurring roles than others. These are the defects that you will have to deal with first. Be familiar with them and do your best to understand the motives behind them, this will allow freedom to come faster.

"Willingness" said, "Never give up on working this process, and at the same time never think that you have arrived. Always strive to get better, do better, and be better."Don't forget to use the "Change" room and your sponsor for help"

"Truth" then joined "Teachable" on his chariot and they rode off into the sunset. "Willingness" and "Humility" flew overhead.

"Was I ready for this?" I thought. Something is telling me that this was going to be another very interesting floor. I picked up the phone and called my boss and told him I would be in soon.

When I arrived on the job it was if nothing had changed, the employees greeted me as if I was there yesterday. I worked as a file clerk and met the people as they entered the building. I gave them paper work to fill out and then sent them to the right department. It was a fairly easy job and my boss was easy to work for, but it was my immediate supervisor that made my life a living hell. In dealing with her the "attitude, resentment and anger" mirrors popped up all day. She didn't like me and I didn't like her. When things slowed down at my desk and these mirrors hovered around me I thought about how to change my attitude, and maybe look at her in a different light, but the mirrors continued to pop up.

At one time during the day mirrors were everywhere. Some were obvious and some were not. According to the "powers that be" in this room, I had a severe attitude problem, even with some of the people that came seeking help. All throughout the day, selfish, self-centered, sabotaging, lazy, conceit, sarcastic, and rude would pop up. It was easy to see and understand why some of these mirrors popped up. However, with some mirrors I had a hard time figuring out why they kept popping up. Selfish, sabotage! I didn't think that selfishness was a part of my makeup. And what was sabotage all about.

As the day went on, and mirrors kept appearing, it was clear to see that I had a lot of work to do on myself. However, for some reason, I was not stressed because of these new found revelations. One thing that this process has been revealing to me is that I was broken when I arrived in this building and many of those character defects have been with me all my life.

After making it back to my apartment I sat on the balcony of my apartment and watched the people go by. I noticed that many people in this neighborhood were involved in this recovery process. Every once in a while someone would walk by with a mirror hovering around beside them. I guess only those involved in the process could see each other's mirrors.

At the gas station on the corner a mirror popped up while a man talked on the phone pumping gas. I saw a lady sitting on the bus stop and a mirror popped up in front of her while she talked to a kid sitting next to her. A couple walking hand in hand down the street and a mirror followed the woman. I laughed because it read "Controlling." Good luck home boy. It was good to see that I was not the only one working my program in Reality Word.

In this world of mirrors, some mirrors did not affect me as much as others, and some I didn't understand why they appeared, such as Lust, hell I'm single! I love girl watching, and spending time with the opposite sex, what's wrong with that? For the past three years I have not been involved with anyone, just some of the smokers around the neighborhood and that came along with the drug. I am definitely going to talk to my sponsor about this one.

The self centered mirror was one of the largest of them all. I wasn't sure why, but at the same time, "It's a dog eat dog world out there, and if you don't look out for yourself who will? That's another one I'll have to share with my sponsor.

Anger, Resentment, Hopeless, Greed, Egotism, Sabotage, and Defensiveness - all of these mirrors kept popping up again and again. "Give me break, I wasn't that bad". The biggest mirror that seemed to stay around the longest was the mirror of Pride. Every time I looked up, this Pride mirror was there. Often times I would just be thinking, and this prideful mirror popped up.

Quickly I found one of those machines to summon my sponsor, and he showed up within minutes. He could see by my demeanor and the look on my face that I was frustrated with this part of the process. Help! This is too much. Laughing he said "calm down many of these behaviors are deeply rooted in your personality and make you who you are today. Some were developed out of your childhood; some are learned behaviors that help you to survive the mean streets you lived in. Some of these character traits are a product of the environment and family structure that you grew up in, while others are just plain old bad habits that you've acquired throughout life."

"Can I fix this, I ask? Again Leon laughed and said "No you can't, but God can". Seeing the real you is not easy. What is there to fix if nothing's broke, this exercise helps you to see you. Then I asked Leon "why was the Pride mirror popping up so. He said "there is not one person who walks through these doors that does not have a problem with Pride. Pride, in fact, is the root of most character defects". So I told him, "My problem is I don't know what it looks like when it shows up?" Leon told me that he could not give me the answer, and I would have to find it for myself. But he did give me a hint, "when you learn to take "I" out of your conversation you will be well on your way." First you will need the correct definitions to some of these defects of character.

He led me to the 2nd floor to the room filled with books, patted me on the back and said, once you get the definition pursue the opposite and you'll be in the ballpark. He turned around and walked away. Why didn't he just tell me the answers, it would have saved me a lot of time. Right then the "lazy" mirror popped up.

First stop, Webster's Dictionary to get a better understanding of this word "pride". The dictionary says people that are prideful think there better that others, and they treat people as if there less than. "Well I have a little of that in me".

Next I look up conceit. Conceit is having a high opinion of yourself; really you think you're something that you're not. "No I don't see this is me, but it could be there". So I moved to egotism. Egotism means you only think about you and your concerns.

So the answer or opposite of Pride and many of my problems is Humility. So I looked up Humility, and found: not proud or arrogant; modest, lowliness, meekness, submissiveness. That can't be it I thought! Sounds like a weakling to me it's got to be a better definition than this. I can't pull this off? I pulled out my Bible to see could I find a better understanding. Psalm 10:4 says *"In their pride the wicked do not seek him; in all their thoughts there is no room for God."* Now that's a dangerous person. They don't think they need God? Then it hit me I use to be that person.

Another scripture was Proverbs 13:10 *"Where there is strife, there is pride, but wisdom is found in those who take advice."* As I look back on my life, it was nothing but strife and drama. According to this scripture, this is where pride lives. In that world, no one listens to anybody. It's a dog eat dog world, every man for himself. The last scripture I found was Proverbs 16:18 *"Pride goes before destruction, a haughty spirit before a fall."* What a sobering thought, according to this I was a walking train wreck, an accident waiting to happen, and it was nobody's fault but mine. Still this word "Humility" was hard to grasp, I couldn't wrap my brain around it to apply it to my life.

I decided to take a break and go to the room called "Change". Maybe I could find some answers there. When I arrived at the room, I looked around for a familiar face but I did not see anyone, so I took a seat up front and waited for the meeting to begin. The leader that day was a distinguished looking gentleman named Jon. You could tell he was well off. He had a 1500 Brook Brothers suit on and I was blinded by the bling from the ring on his finger.

He began by opening the floor for sharing. Many people talked about their character defects and about the challenges they faced while dealing with them. For sure this would not be an overnight fix.

Jon returned to the podium and said "The Devil was once an angel in God's camp and his name was Lucifer or Satan. Not only was he an angel, but he was one of God's chief angels. He was so important that he had angels under him. One day, Satan thought he was equal to God, and told God that he wanted to share his kingdom, quickly Satan was kicked out of heaven and sent to the lowest hell, as a direct result of his Pride". I sat up in my seat when he said that. Jon continued "God laid out his plan for mankind but Satan had another plan and that plan was to lure men away from God. Sin began to take over the world and the only way God could give life to the world again was to send His Son Jesus to Humble Himself and die for the sins of the World."

Then Jon began to tell us how he arrived in this building called "Recovery". To my surprise this meek, mannered man was and still is co-owner of my favorite NFL team. The team was passed down to him from his father. He almost lost everything to drinking, drugs and living wild. Now he is one of the most powerful men in sports history, listening to him, and seeing him you would never know. Today he has 18 years clean and sober and he volunteers by coming to rooms like this and giving back what so freely given to him.

Jon then said something that will forever change my life. He said "the key to reversing all the bad habits you've picked up over the years is learning how to humble yourself, and the best definition for humility that I can give you is strength under control". I almost fell out my seat. That's it I yelled! Everyone in the room turned and looked at me as if I had lost my mind. I didn't care, this definition made sense. You're not weak or a punk when you humble yourself, matter of fact it quite the opposite. It takes a strong man to refrain from proving that you're right, first, or the best in every situation. As long as you know who you are and whose you are, in God your strong! I could have run around the room I was so happy.

At that moment someone sat next to me and gave me a gentle nudge. When I looked up, it was Keith, one of the 12. I had been so focused on this information that I hadn't noticed any of my friends in the room. We shook hands, and he asked me how I was doing. I told him I was doing great now that I know how to deal with this pride inside me. I told Keith I was on the sixth floor, and he told me he was on the seventh. Keith told me he had just entered the 7th floor and anger was his biggest problem. We turned our attention back to Jon who was about to finish sharing. He talked about God in another light. He referred to God as Lord. He said because God is Lord in our lives, He has charge over our lives and He directs us as He sees fit.

He ended the session by thanking and praising God for having all of us in mind when He died for us on that old rugged cross. Just knowing this information gave me inspiration to keep going and to constantly improve. When the meeting ended, we decided to return to our respective floors.

When I returned back to the sixth floor, my mirrors met me at the door but now I looked at them differently. I accepted them and tried to define each mirror that was present in my life.

As the day went on, different mirrors popped up. There was a medium sized mirror that was representative of a "self-centered" behavior, and, of course, the "Pride" and "Selfish" mirrors were still there.

The "Lust" mirror returned and I was upset because I didn't share this with Leon. Immediately I used my card to call him.

When he arrived I shared with him about this "Lust" mirror. Leon told me anything that you put before God will be your God, and this is a problem for most recovering people that come from the lifestyle we came from. He told me not to worry about it. On this floor my job was to recognize it.

For the next few days the "lying" mirror and the "lazy" mirror did not show their faces as much. A new mirror showed up, this was the "sensitive" mirror. People always told me that I was very sensitive, but I never believed them.

Some days were better than others, but some days I felt as if I could not take a step without a mirror appearing to show me what issues I had to confront and deal with. Day in and day out, I was confronted with the real me.

Everyday I went to the room called "CHANGE", and one day, I met two guys that roomed in an apartment building across the street from me. These men had been in *Recovery Tower* for about eight months. At this point, I had been here about nine months.

One of the roommates name was Milton. Milton was an insurance salesman who had a very promising career. Milton said that his father was an alcoholic who died because of his untreated alcoholism. He swore to himself that he would never be like his father; however, that wish did not come true. On the contrary, Milton was just like his dad. He had come to *Recovery Tower* so that he would not die from the same disease his father did.

In the last days before entering *Recovery Tower*, Milton was hanging out with his yuppie buddies on the job. Every day after work he would meet his boss and the rest of his co-workers for happy hour. Milton explained how most of his co-workers would drink for two or three hours before going home, but he would always end up going to another bar drinking himself into a blackout.

Then there was his roommate Mark. He was a college student who had everything going for him. His dad owned the insurance company where Milton worked. Mark was sure to take over the company one day, however, this profession did not peak Mark's interest at all. At this time in his life, all Mark really wanted to do was party and make it through school. Mark however wasn't responsible, nor did he want to be. This is why he was sharing an apartment with Milton.

In the beginning, this living arrangement worked out fine; however, their addictions grew progressively worse, and it was suggested that they both enter *Recovery Tower* together.

The four main mirrors that seemed to show up in Milton's life were "Fear," "Lust," "Pride," and "Unforgiving".

Mark's mirrors were "Pride," "Inconsiderate," "People Pleasing," "Insensitive," "Selfish," "Self-centered," and, of course, "Lust." It seemed like everyone has a problem with some degree of "Lust."

While living on this floor, we turned out to be very good friends. If we were not at work or school, we were going to the room called "CHANGE" or discussing recovery.

We all had been on this floor long enough to know which mirrors popped up continually, and I could not speak for Mark and Milton, but I looked in these mirrors and did not like what I saw.

It was time that I check in with Leon, so I took my sponsor card out and slid it into one of the many slots on this floor. In no time at all Leon showed up and took me to the 3rd floor where I could share with him about these character defects that continued to show up in my life. "Was I really that bad?" He told me that I was on the right track.

The key to this floor was to recognize these character flaws. To figure out how to defeat them would come on the next floor. At this point Leon had to keep reminding me that "recovery" is a life-long process. All we could do is what we could do today and I had the rest of my life to get life right. As we made our way to the elevators, he told me, "Easy does it, but do it."

Attack The Problem

You Got A Fight On Your Hands

Seventh Floor

After the doors opened onto the 7th floor, I noticed that the 6th and the 7th floors were just alike. Everything was the same; nothing had changed. The elevators let me off right outside the same apartment I lived in on the 6th floor. I thought about Mark and Milton and whether or not they had decided to come up to the 7th floor. I walked into my bedroom, and the closest door lit up with my little cartoon character friends: "Truth," "Humility," "Willingness," and "Teachable" appeared on the screen once again.

"Humility" started off by telling me to put the t-shirt on that was lying on the bed. The words on the front of the shirt read "Prayer Changes Things". He told me to pick up the remote control that was lying on the bedroom dresser. I returned to the screen and "Humility" began to explain how to make it successfully through this 7th floor. He said "the key to succeeding on this floor is very simple - understand that you have no power, but God has all power".

"Teachable" chimed in and said, "You have to learn how to take each mirror to God in prayer. Your ultimate goal is to recognize the mirror before it shows up."

"Truth" then said, "Once the mirror shows up, you have to be honest with yourself and do some self examination. You have to recognize the motive behind the behavior that continues to pop up in your life".

"Willingness" jumped in and said, "You have to be willing to change. You can't come into *Recovery Tower* and leave this building the same. If it's a sinful behavior or a bad habit change must come to become a better person.

People that don't like change tend to surround themselves with people that co-sign their behavior. Misery loves company, so be careful of those that are not willing to grow.

Winners come up with a plan that will stop that character defect from raising its ugly head or shut the sin down completely."

The screen went blank and the doorbell rang. I opened the door, and it was Leon. He asked me if I was ready to attack the 7th floor. I told him "yes, as ready as I was going to be."

The doorbell rang again and, to my surprise, it was Mark and Milton. We greeted each other, and I introduced them to Leon.

I noticed that Mark, Milton, and I had on the same t-shirts. They also had the same remote controls in their hands.

I then asked Mark what character defect was giving him the biggest problem and Mark said "Every time I deal with this relationship that I know is no good for me, many mirrors pop up", Leon said "and I bet low self-esteem is one of those mirrors, and Mark said "Yes" how did you know? Leon said because you said it's not good for you. For whatever reason you don't think you deserve better.

When addicted to drugs or alcohol we put up with people, places and things that in a sober state of mind we wouldn't allow.

Leon told us to have a seat while he explained how this process worked here on the 7th floor. He began by saying "The 6th floors main objective is to reveal character defects, take ownership of our behaviors and stop being in denial.

Here at the 7th floor each recovering person's job is to come up with a plan that will minimize or wipe out each character defect that's been revealed.

Some people think it's difficult. They have a hard time believing you can teach old dog new tricks. Some of these behaviors have been with us most of our lives, long before we took our first drink or fix.

If you are born into a dysfunctional family you were taught dysfunction behaviors. Some things will be harder to let go than others.

Then you have those who are in denial about their character defects and bad behavior. These lead a difficult life. What is there to fix if nothing broken. So they continue on hurting themselves and the people around them.

Here on the 7th floor you learn that millions of people have overcome what you are going through. Knowing that your situation is not unique is a blessing. People have been through what you are going through and have overcome.

Here on the 7th floor you will learn how to develop a plan of attack for each character defect that you've identified on the 6th floor. Having a plan and standing firm in your decision to operate that plan is important. Someone once said "Those that fail to plan, plan to fail". The plan that you comprise for each defects of character has to be readily available to use when these defects of character show up.

Recognizing why they show up will be equally as important. Examining yourself, going to meetings and spending time with your sponsor will help you in this area.

Leon then reached into his back pocket and pulled out a remote similar to ours. He closed his eyes for a few second and when he opened them there was a "self-centred" mirror hovering above his head. He closed his eyes again and said "Lord please forgive me for my thoughts" he then opened his eyes pointed the remote towards the "self-centred" mirror, pushed a button and a beam of light came out and destroyed the mirror.

"The key to overcoming these character defects is thinking first, and not reacting first. Second you pray about the situation. This give you time to think about the plan that you've already thought about. After praying and believing, take the remote and point it toward the mirror and push the button.

Once the button is pushed, a beam of light will destroy the mirror. Then he put a twist on what seemed like a simple process. He said that the mirror would break only if you are serious about changing for good. I was not certain about anyone else, but "How would you know if you are serious or not?"

At that moment, Milton's cell phone rang and out of respect, Milton moved away from us, reached into his pocket, and answered the phone. Immediately his whole demeanor changed. As he listened to the person on the other end of this call, Milton was completely silent but it was easy to see he was getting upset. From what we could gather from the conversation, it appeared that someone from his job was giving him some bad news. When he finished his conversation and hung up the phone, he told us that the person on the phone was a co-worker.

This person had just come out of a special meeting at the job where a laptop computer had come up missing. The supervisor believed it was one of three people who had stolen the laptop. The main suspects were Milton, the guy on the phone, and a guy who worked in the mailroom.

Milton told us that he had not stolen the laptop in question and he resented the fact that he was being accused. As he began to explain to us where he was the last time he saw the laptop, he was slowly, but surely getting very upset.

By the time Milton finished talking, mirrors were popping up all around him and Milton seemed not to care. Swearing, anger, frustration, and resentment mirrors to name a few were popping up.

As these mirrors surrounded Milton, he picked up the remote and pointed it towards one of the mirrors, then pushed the button; however, nothing happened. Again, Milton pointed the remote control at another mirror and pushed the button and still nothing. He rapidly pushed the button, but nothing happened.

Out of frustration, he threw the remote to the floor and yelled; "Now this thing doesn't work, what else can go wrong?" Leon picked up the remote and said, "There is nothing wrong with your remote, but there is something wrong with how you are using it."

With fire in his eyes, Milton said, "What could I possibly be doing wrong?" Leon said, "You are trying to do this in your own power." He grabbed Milton by the arm and led him to a large picture mirror on the dresser. Milton could see that the t-shirts read, "Prayer changes things."

Instead of leaning on your own understanding, you have to learn how to take everything to God in prayer. Leon gave Milton the remote.

We could still see all the mirrors surrounding Milton who bowed his head and asked us to join in with him in prayer. We all bowed are heads silently agreeing with Milton as he prayed.

He asked God to forgive him for reacting without thinking, and he apologized for not trusting God in the first place. He prayed for the situation at work and all whom were involved, and Milton prayed that the laptop would resurface, or they would find the person who took it.

When he finished, he raised his head, pointed the remote at the mirror called "anger", and pushed the button. That's when a red beam of light came from the remote and shattered the mirror into a million little pieces. Before the glass could hit the floor, it all disappeared. Milton then turned to the rest of the mirrors, prayed, and destroyed the remaining mirrors.

We all were amazed at the process we had just witnessed, but we could tell Milton was still upset about his job situation. Leon reminded us about the "powerless concept". He explained to us that most people who never get into recovery think they have the power to overcome their character defects. As a result, they struggle through life always falling short. So as soon as we say, "We can't", God smiles and says, "I know you can't but I can".

We cannot change people, places or things. We cannot change what people say, think, or do. What we can change is how we react to each situation.

In everything we go through, God knows we will go through it before it happens. So God is waiting on us to call on him about a situation that He already knows about and has allowed to happen.

Then, he quoted a scripture in the Bible saying, *"Trust in the Lord with all thine heart and lean not to thine own understanding, in all thy ways acknowledge him and he will direct thy path."*

He, then said, "Think first before you react and, "yes", it's okay to be angry, but don't react."

Leon then said he had to leave but before he left, he turned to Milton and said, "There were two mirrors that never showed up when you lost your temper, and these mirrors were "Liar" & Thief". So what are you worried about? We all looked at each other and gave each other high-fives as he left the room.

We sat down and started discussing this part of our recovery. We decided that before we attack the rest of the day, we would list the top 10 defects of character that we noticed in our lives. Since pride was the mother of them all, we put that at the top of the list to conquer.

As we went over our list of mirrors, it was plain to see that some of these character flaws had been with us for most of our lives. It was surely going to take an all-powerful God to remove such monsters in our lives.

Now that we have identified the top ten character defects, the next thing for us to do is to figure out what causes them, when do they show up. And lastly come up with a plan to eliminate them from our lives.

Today, we see the problem and the problem begins and ends with us. Up until now, these character defects have been showing up in our lives anytime they wanted to. The character defect acted as the puppeteer and we are the puppets; doing and acting however it wanted us to act. "Well enough is enough", and we were willing to fight for our new lives today.

The hour was getting late, and we all knew that we still had a lot of work ahead of us in the days ahead. Before Milton and Mark left, we prayed and encouraged each other.

That next morning, before my feet hit the floor, my knees hit the floor. I am convinced that this is a ritual I will do for the rest of my life. After prayer, I showered, got dressed, and headed out.

I had the day off, so I thought it would be good to visit my parents' house.

On my way to my parents' house, I had a hard time passing up the coffee shop. As I entered, I could see I wasn't the only person that could not pass it up. The coffee shop was packed that morning, so I waited patiently in line. As I stood in line waiting to be served, the person that was taking everyone's order obviously was having a bad day. She was rude to her co-workers and rude to an elderly man who had already ordered his coffee and was waiting patiently for his order to come up.

By the time I got to the front of the line, the older gentleman was still waiting and had not, yet, received his coffee. He politely got the coffee attendants attention and reminded her again about his coffee and once again she was very rude to him, and the young lady even questioned whether or not he had even ordered. Visibly distraught, the man put his head down and went to the back of the line. Any other time, I would have jumped in her face and asked to see her manager, but because I am trying to change, I prayed for the sister and then I ordered my coffee and the old man's coffee as well. After paying for both of the coffees, I left the coffee shop feeling pretty good almost as if I had passed a test or something similar.

When I arrived at my parents' home, my sister and her husband were also there. When I was out using and abusing drugs, my sister was the one person I could always go to and talk to about anything. Up until this day, I always thought she was someone who understood me and was someone whom I could trust.

As the day went on, my sister and I found our selves alone in the den discussing everything under the sun when her husband called her from the kitchen. She had just walked out of the room towards the kitchen when she realized that she had left her purse in the room unattended with me. She stopped in her tracks, came back into the room, and tried to nonchalantly retrieve her purse. She could not look me in the eye as she left the room this second time.

I never felt so bad in my entire life. "How could she? I have never taken anything from her." The pain of her action began to consume my whole mind and body.

Mirrors began to pop up. "Anger – Resentment, Guilt, Low self worth" and, before I knew it, I was having my own pity party. I didn't feel like praying, meditating – nothing at all. I just wanted to leave. I even thought about a drink and this is the first time that's happen since I entered *Recovery Tower*.

I made it to the front door without anyone seeing me, and quietly left. The urge to take a drink hit me like a ton of bricks. As I stepped out my parent's house I notice a box outside the door to summon Leon. I reached in my pocket and put the card in the slot.

Within minutes Leon showed up. I told him what happen and how I was feeling, and I even considered taking a drink. He suggested that we go to the room called "Change", and so we did. We found 2 seats in the back of the room. I had a hard time lifting my head. All I could think about was my sister's reaction.

The instructor approached the podium and said his name was Cash. He was about 35 years old and wore baggie jeans, tennis shoes and had dreadlocks down to his shoulder; he also spoke with a Jamaican accent. Cash shared he got married at 18 years old and by that time we was an alcoholic in denial.

By the time he turned 20 he had one daughter and a kid on the way. The whole time he was married all he and his wife did was fight and argue. Most of it was because of his drinking. One day in a drunken rage he packed his bags and left and for 12 years he never communicated with his family. During that time he found out that he had a son, but never made any attempts to see his family. He now had 3 years clean and sober and for 2 years he's tried to reconcile with his family. His wife was able to get a divorce and never remarried. She didn't mind Cash coming back into their lives but the kids wanted nothing to do with him.

They planned to meet at his son's high school football game. This would be the first time he saw his son, who was also named Cash Jr. After the game he waited with anticipation for Cash to come out of the locker room. Not knowing what to expect when his son saw him standing there with his mom he knew who he was. They looked just alike. Cash Jr. even wore dreadlocks.

Cash Jr. walked up to him and cussed him out and told him he never wanted to see him again. His daughter was also there and they both turned and walked away. Cash then said "the first thing I wanted to do was get high" I look at Leon and said "that's the very first thing I wanted to do". Cash then said "but that would have added to my problem. Instead I surround myself with people that are just like me right here in the room called "Change".

People in the rooms of recovery told me to begin to pray about the situation and pray for my kids. He then said "one of the best things that I learned during that very difficult time was "What part did I have to play in that situation. I learned that they had every right to be upset with me, and if they never spoke to me again I'd have to deal with it. I also learned that drinking and using was not an option. He's also had some good news; just recently he and his kids are talking.

That was all I needed to hear. I lean over to Leon and said "This is the medicine I needed."

I return back to my parent's home and made my way to the bathroom. I looked at these mirrors that hovered around me and began to asset each mirror and ask the question "what part did I play in allowing my sister to react in that manner."

With the Anger and Resentment who was I mad at my sister because she was doing what I would have done? Or was I embarrassed because my life has come to this point where I put my family in a position to where they have to protect themselves because they couldn't trust me.

I took a deep breath knowing I would not be able to run from this problem. With mirrors still surrounding me I look at myself in the bathroom mirror. Fighting this urge to have pity party, I asked myself if I deserved this, or did I bring this on myself? I asked God to free me of these feelings I was experiencing.

After saying a quick prayer, I finally looked up and the guilt mirror that was staring me in my face. It was as if this mirror was trying to bring me down, but I had come too far to let this happen. At that moment, I began asking God not to let guilt steal my joy. I had a long way to go and by talking to God I began to encourage myself, constantly reminding myself how far I had come since I entered this building called Recovery. With the remote in my hand, I destroyed the guilt mirror.

I then turned to the "low-self worth" mirror and rebuked that thought in the name of Jesus. I closed my eyes and asked God to strengthen me and help me to remember who I was in Him. Then I took the remote and destroyed that mirror as well.

Looking in the bathroom mirror I could see the anger, resentment and selfish mirror hovering behind me. I was angry and I wanted to stay angry. The ironic part was I did not know whom I was angry with, me or my sister. She has a right to protect herself and her valuables.

After a few minutes of looking into that mirror, I finally asked myself how I would have handled that situation. Would I have left something valuable in the room with a known addict or left my valuables in the room showing that person I trusted him or her? This was a no brainier. I would have came back to get my valuables just as my sister did. On the contrary, even with all of this knowledge knowing that I was handling this situation wrong it did not make me feel any better.

There was a hole deep down in my gut and there was nothing I could do about filling it. I asked God to forgive me for how I was feeling and to help me through this process. I pointed the remote at the anger mirror and fired watching the mirror shatter into a thousand pieces.

The next mirror was "resentment". At this point, I was willing to let go, even though the hurt was still present. In order for me to get closure in this situation, I knew I would have to face my sister and let her know that it was my fought and not hers. Once again, I asked God to give me the strength to overcome my feelings, and I blasted the mirror and turned to the last remaining mirror which was selfishness.

It was clear to me that I was only concerned about me. I didn't think about what my sister was going through or how she felt. I knew she loved me, but the feelings inside me took over and I could only think about me and how I felt. In times like these, I didn't care about anyone else but myself. I asked God to forgive me for being so selfish and I prayed for His continued help. I then pointed the remote at the last remaining mirror and blasted it.

I walked out of the bathroom and joined the rest of my family in the kitchen area. Still my sister could not look me in the eyes. She knew she had hurt me, and I could see that it was really changing the mood in the house. It is customary in my family to say nothing and act as if things don't happen. There could be an elephant in the room and if it made someone in my family uncomfortable no one would mention it. As the day went on, I tried to make her feel at ease by laughing and joking. Regardless of how much we both tried to disguise our feelings, the tension was still there.

Finally, I could see that I was making her very uncomfortable. She politely made up an excuse to leave, picked up her purse and made her way toward the bedroom to get her coat.

I felt so bad knowing that the tension in the house was being caused by me. I followed her into the bedroom and asked her to forgive me. She looked up with tears in her eyes and apologized for not trusting me. I smiled and told her that I would have done the same thing. We both laughed and embraced each other and returned to the kitchen together with the rest of our family.

What a day. I learned so much about myself as a result of that situation, and I knew that I would see these mirrors again in the future. I knew I had a long way to go before I am fully recovered, but now, today, I do it one day at a time.

After spending time with my family, I made my way back to the room called "CHANGE". I took a seat in the back of the room and thought about this uphill battle I was facing. I turned my attention to the speaker who was wrapping up her time at the podium. I only heard a little of the speaker's message, but what I heard summed up my task at hand. She said, "Give yourself a break, Rome wasn't built in a day." That's it, I thought. My life has been broken for a long time. It will take an all powerful God to fix this. At that moment, it registered like a bolt of lightning and sense of calm came over me. When they told us to pray, I've been praying because they told me to, but today I know I have too. I need a power greater than myself, and there is no way in the world I can change my life.

That next morning, I woke up feeling like a million dollars. What a great day I had yesterday. The episode at my parents' house began the healing with my family in conjunction with the "bomb" that was dropped in my spirit in the room called "CHANGE". There is not one individual on earth who can single-handedly change his or her own life. We all need a power greater than ourselves, and that power is God.

I climbed out of bed and could hardly wait to get down on my knees to pray. Today, I was willing to turn it over to God. (What a load off.)

I slowly started getting the hang of being on this floor. Mirrors still popped up but with each passing day I was learning more and more about me. I learned to think before speaking, which really helps me in the area of being sarcastic and disrespecting others. It also helped me with my attitude. Don't get me wrong, I am far from being healed from my character defects, but with this new revelation, a light is at the end of the tunnel" was visible for sure. There were still some areas in my life that I had a hard time recognizing as being problematic, and the "Selfish" mirror was one that seemed to always pop up in my life.

One day while at work, I got some great news. I was up for a manager's position, which would increase my pay considerably. Management told me that they were considering me seriously for the position as well as another co-worker named Dave, who was a good friend of mine. I heard though the grapevine that one of the problems some supervisors had with Dave was his excessive tardiness. Dave and I talked about this new position and we decided that whatever the outcome, we would not let it come between our friendships.

One morning on my way to work, I saw Dave on the side of the road with the hood up on his car. I drove right by him knowing that he had a problem with being late to work. I got to work about five minutes before the day started knowing Dave would not make it to work on time. I happened to be standing with the boss when Dave walked in 15 minutes late. When I walked back into my office, a "Selfish" mirror popped up. I looked into this mirror and questioned its reason for being there. I didn't do anything to make Dave late for work. He is a grown man just like I am. Two mirrors popped up, "Denial and Justify". I knew I was supposed to pray and then zap these mirrors, but I wanted Leon to see these mirrors first before I followed suit because surely this was a mistake.

When Leon showed up, I thought he was going to agree with me, but not only did he not agree with me, he added "Lack of Trust" to the picture. I sat down to hear his explanation. He said in a very calm, simplistic way, "If I trust God, then nothing could stop me from getting this promotion." Then Leon ask me a question, "If God has already ordained this position for you, who or what could stop it? I thought Dave was your friend?" I replied, "He is." He then said, "If Dave is your friend, you knew that management was unhappy with Dave for being late. Not only did he loose points toward his being in the running to obtain the Manager position, but in addition, he could lose his job.

How could I be so selfish? Not only could he lose his job, but also Dave had twin baby girls! After Leon left, I turned and those mirrors were still there. I asked God to forgive me and then I also prayed for Dave, that he would not lose his job. I took the remote and blasted the two mirrors.

I turned and went into the room called "CHANGE" and took a seat. This part of the building was no joke. I was tired of me. One day I could be up and the next day down.

In the room called "CHANGE", the facilitator asked if I would like to share. I really did not want to but I knew God was guiding my steps. I had no idea what I was going to say, but as I stood behind the podium and looked out into the audience, tears began to well up in my eyes. I started sharing with everyone how I felt like a man who looked in the mirror and was unhappy with what he saw. I asked the group to pray for me then I took my seat. Everyone began to clap and pat me on the back. Still, this did not make me feel any better. Leon joined me, and told me that I was right on track. I looked at him as if he were crazy. He reminded me that I did not become broken in a day and it was surely going to take more than a day for me to be restored. He then told me that deep down inside he knew I wanted to get better and my wanting to get better was enough for God. The key is once you fall; learn how to get back up. I returned to my apartment where Mark and Milton were waiting for me. I shared my experience with them and it seemed as if they had been through just as much as I had.

That day and the days to follow turned out to be very challenging for all of us. We were dead-set on getting better. It all goes back to the age-old question, "Can an old dog learn new tricks?" "Yes. He can!" is the answer; however, it all depends on whether or not some very key ingredients are present: humility, staying teachable, willingness, and honesty. Studying the Word of God coupled with prayer changes both how we think and how we behave.

Milton said "a few minutes with God is more powerful than a lifetime of counselling". In the beginning the mirrors showed up, we prayed, and destroyed the mirrors. As we grew, we learned to pray before the mirror showed up, and God would always give us alternatives to our actions just as The Bible says. *He will make a way for you to escape.*

Mark had a different observation. He talked about how everything around us seemed to have changed. People were nicer; family was loving and tolerant. In all actuality, this really was not the case. Because of what we've learned here in *Recovery Tower* we have changed, and we see life different.

We talked about the work that still needed to be done and how dangerous it is to think that we have arrived, or to think we are completely well. Mark said, "Until Jesus comes back; we will be working on ourselves, meaning that we are all works in progress." Those who think they have arrived or think they are well have added a couple more character defects to their lists, with delusion topping the charts then denial. Those who do not want to work on themselves become lazy, or they sit in the seat next to God thinking they are virtually faultless. Mark then quoted a scripture, *"No man is perfect, no not one"*.

Mark turned to me and said "I always expected God to miraculously do the work for me. I expected God to hit me with this spiritual lightning bolt and I would never drink or use again. It's not that God can't do it, but what would we learn? God has delivered people from drug and alcohol addiction with one touch and many never return to drinking or using. But for many of us He saw something deeper and more dangerous that the drugs. He saw our Pride.

I truly believe that recovery was divinely put in place, here on earth by God for people like you and me that was to prideful and selfish to receive what God has for us. Milton then said "Many times I thought I was healed but my actions before I took a drink or a hit was far from what God want me to be." Your right I said, I had to be taught freedom; I had to be taught how to walk in my deliverance. Once you come through these doors drugs and alcohol is a very small part of our problem.

It was time to move on to the next floor, but before we did we all decided to go back to the room called "CHANGE". As we took our seats, the facilitator open the floor for sharing and a young lady who was sitting in the front row raised her hand quickly. She approached the podium and said "My name is Danyell and I have a problem with drinking and using. I've been divorce 2 years as a direct result to my drinking and using. I am barely holding on to my job as a science teacher at a local high school, and this is my second time coming to *Recovery Tower.*"

What she said made me sit up in my seat. Again I was reminded that just because you go through this process you don't make it.

"I thought I was too smart to become an addict, but my drinking and using progressively got worse and I found myself looking for help, here, in *Recovery Tower* again. I only surrendered because my family put so much pressure on me. They were overjoyed when I entered the program but I never surrendered to the process. While I was here the first time I only made it to the second floor before I convinced myself I was not like everybody else.

This time I am determined to go all the way. The sixth and seventh floors reveal things about me that I never knew existed. Now I know why my husband left me. Now, I know what the Bible means when it says *"My people are destroyed from lack of knowledge"*

Danyell then gave us a hint, she said, "It may be difficult in the beginning, but as you grow and learn how to humble yourself, you will see the power in humility. Humbling yourself will be one of your biggest weapons used to fight 90% of your character defects. Humility is the oil in the engine that keeps the motor running smooth. Humbling yourself will be the key to a better life while this change takes place.

I leaned over and asked Milton, "Humble yourself, how do you do that?" Mark overheard me and said, "Where I come from people that humble themselves are considered punks."

Danyell must have sensed that people had questions because she then posed the very same question that we were all asking, "Does anyone here know the definition of being humble?" Hands began to ggo up and many people had different definitions and interpretations of what humble meant. The best definition,, however, travelled from the back of the room, and to my surprise, it was by Shorty. He stood up and said "I use to think meek and humble people were wimps and punks because that's what the neighbourhood.

Today, however, I've learned that I was wrong. I searched far and wide for a definition that I could live with, one that I could apply to my life. Finally I settled with "strength under control." I don't have to be first, the best, recognized, I don't have to be right all the time, or the best, humility keeps me in the right state of mind. Mark looked at me and said, "Now I can live with that." I gave in a high five and said, I believe I can work with that." I had to laugh because there is no room for "I" in being humble).

When the meeting ended, I made a beeline over to Shorty. We embraced and I introduced Shorty to Mark and Milton. We talked about how this building was changing our lives for the better. I was surprised to hear that Shorty was just heading to the seventh floor. Shorty said he was in no hurry, and he was taking his time this time. We made it to our individual elevators and said our goodbyes to each other.   I pushed the "up" button and the door opened.

As I entered the elevator and the doors closed behind me, I gazed out of this glass elevator and I could see that there were fewer elevators going up. As we traveled up through the clouds, the sun's rays filled the elevator and a rainbow settled in the distance as each color glimmered off the backdrop of a never-ending navy blue sky. As the elevator slowly inched its way upward, I realized that this was surely the longest ride yet. I thought about Shorty's answer when he said, "He was taking his time this time." Of course, I questioned my own pace as I progressed through this building.

Not far from the elevator that I was riding in, there was another elevator that was slowly coming down. The person inside was standing facing me as both elevators passed each other, I could see that the person in the elevator was Carmen.

She looked right at me but I don't think she saw me as she looked right through me. I wave at her but she turned her head, maybe she did see me or she was embarrassed. I felt so helpless as I watched her elevator travel downward, I thought about her kids and her private practice. I said a prayer for her and her family. I prayed that God would never leave her nor forsake her. I watched her elevator as it disappeared through the clouds below when realized that I was headed into the area that she had just left. The top of her elevator read, "NOT WILLING TO CHANGE – NOT WILLING TO SURRENDER".

What Part Did You Play In it?

Eighth Floor

As the elevator came to a halt, a sign blinked on inside and it read "Where There Is Smoke, There is Fire." I've been in this building for almost ten months now, and I knew that something weird was about to happen.

I bowed my head and prayed "God continue to guide me" and I thanked Him in advance for what was about to happen. As I raised my head, and looked out into this beautiful sky filled with elevators, I said to myself, "Let's Do This!"

Before I could get the words out of my mouth, the doors opened. The smell of smoke was thick in the air. The doors opened onto a small hill that overlooked a valley surrounded by mountains. Down in the valley, there was a large lake, and from what I could see in and around the lake, fires were burning out of control.

I looked to the right of me and I could see another elevator sitting afar off on top of another hill similar to the elevator I was on. A person like myself just walked out of the elevator and was headed down into her own personal valley. I could see smoke coming from the center of the valley where she was walking. I wish I could tell you that I was ready to run down into this valley and attack the next part of this process, but instead, fear was growing inside of me. I bowed my head again and prayed to God and asked

Him to guide and protect me as I continued on this journey to total recovery.

There was a trail that led down into this smoked filled valley. As I started making my way down, there was a fork in the road that led to the room called "CHANGE". Couldn't hurt! So I turned and went inside. It turned out to be a good decision, because Shorty was in the room. I pulled him aside and shared with him that I was still having a problem with seeing Carmen going down in the elevator, and there was no better person to talk to than Shorty.

I asked him "Why would a person return to that type of hell." Shorty told me that he was sad to hear about Carmen and he remembered the day he had to take the elevator down.

"When I first walked into this building five years ago, I thought I'd never use again, but because I did not surrender completely to this process, I fell through my own personal trap door that took me deeper into the pit of hell."

He then smiled and said, "But God is good, and He gave me another chance. I can't speak for Carmen, but my problem boils down to being totally honest, especially on the sixth and seventh floors. This is why I'm taking my time. I have a problem with all four of the main character defects that automatically thrust me into relapse mode.

I also had a problem being "powerless." Becoming powerless and gaining all power" did not register for a long time.

Today, however, is a different story. The concept makes perfect sense. The power that is given to me is God's power and we sometimes get it twisted by thinking we have power, and once that happens, we enter onto a destructive road. From that point on, it's only a matter of time before I was using and abusing drugs and alcohol again.

As he continued talking, my mind drifted away thinking about these four character defects. For the life of me, I could not name them. It was eating me up inside. While Shorty was still talking, I blurted out "What four main character defects?" Shorty laughed and said, "There is so much information to learn in recovery that it is impossible to remember it all. This is one of the reasons we continue going to the room called "CHANGE". The four main character defects most addicts/alcoholics walk through the door with are *Pride, Sexual Misconduct, Selfishness, and Resentment*. A person that avoids these four defects will without a doubt release the monster inside called addiction.

He told me it was time he'd get back to the seventh floor, he was still having problems with his many character defects or mirrors popping up in his life. He gave me a quick hug and then headed back to the 7th floor.

After talking to Shorty, I decided to continue back to the eighth floor. I took the trail that led me down to what appeared to be a large lake. The whole time I was walking down the trail, I was wondering if I had left the seventh floor too early. I also thought about Carmen, she had a big time problem with the powerless concept. Then I remembered what Ndey said *Some must die that others may live*, what a cold blooded saying. I pray I don't get stuck holding on to a part of my life that will not let me change. I'm not giving up on Carmen; just like Shorty came back Carmen can too. I knew I had to press on for me. The closer I got to the lake, the thicker the smoke became.

The lake was about as long as two football fields. There were at least ten or twelve bridges that connected the two sides and there were fires burning on all of them. At the end of each bridge on the other side of the lake, there was someone sitting at what looked like a desk, but the smoke was so thick I couldn't make out who these people were.

Some of the bridges were charred completely. Some were nearly destroyed while others looked like they'd not been burning very long at all. As I stood there, not knowing what to do, Leon walked up to me (Thank God) and said "each person on the other side of the lake is someone special in your life, it could be a family member, or a friend but whoever it is this person is close enough to have a special connection with you. Most likely in your drinking and using you harmed them either mentally or physically.

Immediately I felt a pain in the bottom of my gut. I hurt so many people, in my addiction. I stole, lied, and cheated so much so that I probably forgot most of the people and the incidents. With tears in my eyes I look at Leon and said "I don't know if I'm up to this".

As we walked down to the edge of the water "Leon said remember the process of recovery is not here to hurt you, but no one said it would be easy. It takes courage to get better, to change, and to right the wrongs that you've caused". As we approached the edge of the water there was a desk, a chair, and a keyboard positioned at the end of each bridge. There was also a button with the word "SEND" on each desk.

The tops of the desks were made of glass and they looked like computer monitors. A picture of the person sitting on the other side of the lake will be on the screen. The first picture on the screen was my father. As I looked across the lake, I could barely see him because the smoke was so thick.

The bridge was almost sixty percent gone, and a pretty good size fire was still burning on the bridge. As it continued to burn, parts of this bridge began to fall, splashing into the water. All of a sudden, my knees got weak and my heart seemed to skip a beat. Leon put his arm around me and said, "Here on this floor, your job is to type out how you assisted in destroying each relationship. There is one thing you need to know about this computer it will only input what you did, not what that person did to you. What part did you play in destroying this relationship?"

I started to think about the things that I had done to my father, and what an embarrassment I had become. I pulled the keyboard close to my lap and began to type. I saw my words appear on the desktop screen. I started off by apologizing for being so disobedient. I also apologized for breaking the rules in his house and not respecting his authority. As I continued typing, I wrote about how I thought he did not spend enough time with me, indicating how hurt I was. He never showed up to see my football and basketball games as a kid. But when I looked at the screen to see what I had typed, the screen went blank and the words "What Part Did You Have to Play in It?" flashed across the screen. Leon looked at the screen and said, "Remember this is not about what they did to you, it will only record what you did to them." He also said that every time I get off track, the computer will automatically stop typing your words. They will start again when you continue writing about the part you played in the destruction of the relationships."

There was something else special about this computer. Every time I came across a situation and was unable to remember all the details, the computer took over like a self-playing piano. It even brought up some incidents that I had long forgotten. Maybe because I was too drunk or too high to remember what happened or maybe I purposely tried to erase these memories from my mind.

Some arguments were certainly not my fault, but no matter how hard I tried to justify my actions, the computer would not accept any of my accusations. Some incidents I tried to skip over, but the computer overrode my desires. In my dad's attempt to help me and me being so hard headed we almost got into some physical altercations. I was the one that disrespected his house. I was the one that didn't listen, I was the one that stole from him, and lied.

In trying to finish writing about the confrontations with my dad I had to sometimes take a break from this process by walking along the shore. Determine to get through this I press on.

I finally put a period behind this part of the process with my dad and the part I played in the destruction of that relationship. Once I had finish writing, I pushed the "SEND" button. After a few seconds, the screen flashed, "ACCEPTED." "Who accepted this information?" I thought to myself, did this mean my dad accepted it? Or did this computer accept it? Where did it go? The computer flashed another sign. "Please Move to The Next Bridge."

On my way to the next bridge, I noticed a path that lead to the room called "CHANGE". This was a good idea. After what I'd just gone through, I was in no hurry to deal with the rest of my family and whoever else was on the other side of the lake.

I entered the room called "CHANGE", first looking for some familiar faces, but I saw no one I knew. Once the meeting got started and the facilitator made her way to the podium, she introduced herself as Hunter.

Hunter was a nice looking Polynesian woman who had been clean and sober 6 years. She had a tattoo of a reef on her wrist and a flower in her hair. She said "I've been divorced for over 2 years now and my ex-husband and I lost our kids to the system because of our using and abusing drugs. It's been a long hard battle and I am in the last phase of getting my children back."

After talking about her past, she began to talk about this process called recovery. She started talking about the many promises we as addicts and alcoholics break while in our addiction and how our loved ones had a right not to trust us. "In the beginning, we were really sincere when we said we would never use drugs again, or we sincerely believed we would pay back the money we borrowed.

Deep down inside, we really wanted to keep the promises we made with our loved ones, but most of the time these arrangements ended up in more broken promises. Then there were times we knew we were lying and never intended to pay back the debts we owed. In our disease we did whatever it took to get the next hit, fix, or drink and nothing or no one was excluded.

Lying became a part of my life, and it was as easy as drinking water. I lied so much that I had a hard time separating what was real or fantasy. To get caught in a lie didn't mean much to me and if I got caught I just move on.

As I sat there listening, I identified with everything she was saying. I was that person who would lie, cheat, and steal at the drop of a hat in order to get what I wanted. Addiction turned me into an out-of-control monster and if this program couldn't help me, I was in big trouble.

After Hunter finished sharing, she asked if anyone had a burning desire to share. A young lady sitting behind me raised her hand. As she walked to the podium, you could tell she had been crying and said "hi my name is Donna and I have a problem with drugs and alcohol. I can't believe I choose drinking and using over my kid's safety and well being. I would leave them in the house for days without coming home. This drug is the most powerful thing I've ever encountered and I wish I'd never started using it. Thank God for my 14 year old who knew how to take care of my 7-year-old and 4-year-old. My kids are staying with my mother while I'm here in *Recovery Tower*. I'm not sure if my kids even want to see me again." I wish I could say I would never use again, but I know I'd be lying to myself. I hate drinking I hate using but my hate for it has nothing to do with the power that comes over me. Somebody please help me! Donna could not hold back the tears any longer and went back to her seat. There was not a dry eye in the house. It is amazing how sometimes we think our situation is the worse until you hear what someone else is going through.

Hunter returned to the podium and said "if you can remember one thing while here in this process called recovery, please remember this, God didn't bring you this far to let you go. God could have let you suffer and die in the state you were in but right in the nick of time he rescued you." That seemed like a good word to leave on so after the meeting was over I headed back to the eight floor.

As I made my way to the next bridge, I could see that this bridge was about fifty percent demolished. As I sat down at the desk, the screen lit up and my mother's picture flashed across the screen. I figured it would be her. I took a deep breath and picked up the keyboard and put it in my lap. Where would I start? I promised her that I would quit drinking and using so many times that after a while I just stopped making promises. There was no one on this earth I had hurt more than my mother, and this was going to be difficult. Slowly I began to write what I was thinking and feeling, beginning from as far back as I could remember to the present. Once again, I apologized for the wrong I had done and the harm I caused. I apologized for the TV and VCR that came up missing when I staged a break-in at her house to support my addiction. I apologized for stealing her car while she was at the market. I told her that I had a spare key and I took her car to pay off a debt I owed. After looking at those two disgusting incidents, I had to get up from the desk again and take a walk as I was extremely disappointed in myself for hurting my mother.

I walked down to the edge of the water and looked up at the bridge that was burning out of control. Then I looked across the lake and I could barely see my mother through all the smoke. I decided I was not going to let my past behavior break us up, so I turned and went back to the desk.

I started typing without stopping as if I was in a zone. Tears streamed down my face as I trudged through the pain of putting all of these hurtful things down on paper. My mother, the person I loved more than anyone in this world, I treated her worse than a stranger on the street.

All of her friends knew what I had become and I had become an embarrassment to her. She stopped playing cards with her friends because they said things about me that she didn't like. Every keystroke rattled my mind, body, and soul. I knew I had to finish this paper, and if my mother gives me another chance, I will do my best to make it up to her.

When I finally finished writing and before I pushed send, I prayed to God that my mother would give me another chance. I pushed the "SEND" button and quickly it came back "ACCEPTED." I slumped down in the seat and thanked God that it was over. I got up and ran to the room called "CHANGE". I stayed in that room for two hours and afterwards I was ready to move forward. This room called "CHANGE" saved my life and there was no way I could have made it this far without these rooms.

After leaving the room called "CHANGE", I made my way back to the lake. The third bridge I walked up to was ninety percent gone, and it looked like a three-alarm fire. The flames were reaching high into the sky, and I wondered who could this be?

I walked over to the desk, and saw it was by ex-fiancée Gail. "Oh my God this is not good". I used and abused this girl more than anyone else. She was with me at the height of my addiction. She would sometimes put me to bed when I was too drunk to do it myself. She cleaned up behind me when my dinner ended up on the floor. I took her money, her jewelry, and anything else I could sell to support my habit. But most of all, I stole her heart.

Before Gail met me, she was a nice church-going girl who had dreams and aspirations. She had her first sexual experience with me and, after that, she fell deeply in love with me. I told her that I loved her, but I really didn't. Come to think of it, I am not sure if I knew what love really was. I was so caught up in my drinking and using that everything else was a distant second.

At that time, I used Gail and other women as well to get what I wanted from them. I even turned Gail on to drugs and alcohol and a lifestyle that she probably never would have experienced if I had not come into her life. Before her drinking and using cross the line into addiction, she sought help from the church and God delivered her with one touch. Immediately, her first order of business was to get rid of me.

I sat down in the chair and began to write. Truthfully, I really was not under the impression that she would ever forgive me. If I was to put myself in her shoes, I am not sure that I could forgive me. Even though forgiveness is part of a Christian's walk, I believe she had the right not to forgive me. I would not be upset with her if this was her choice.

After hours of writing, stopping and starting, walking and praying, I sometimes wondered if it was worth it, but I kept pressing on. Once again, I prayed; however, this time I did not pray for Gail to forgive me. I prayed that God would heal Gail's heart. I prayed that God would have His way in her life. I hit the "Send" button and I sat there waiting for a response, but nothing happened. I decided to go to the room called "CHANGE". Thank God for this room called "CHANGE" - my safe haven, my hiding place, my peace in the midst of a storm.

When I returned to the lake, there were many bridges still on fire. Some were blazing infernos and other fires had just begun to ignite.

From the man at the corner store that took a chance with me by giving me a job and I turned around and stole so much from him that he had to fire me, to my nieces and nephews to whom I promised birthday presents and I never showed up at their parties. Then there were all the women that I used and abused.

I examine each and every relationship and look at what part I played in the destruction of that relationship. I felt so low I had to get on a ladder to see the bottom. After going through this process, I truly understood what being humbled meant.

Off in the distance there was one bridge left but there was no fire on this bridge which made no sense. From what I could see there was a computer table at the edge of water just like all the rest. Was this someone that I was getting ready to hurt or what? Curiosity got the best of me so I went over to table at the end of the bridge and turned the monitor on. Low and behold a picture of my grandfather popped on the screen. Like being hit with a upper-cut I had to sit down.

My grandfather had passed 4 years ago. In the last 2 years of his life he came to live with us before he passed away. He was also my best friend. As a kid he uses to take me to ball games, and when I played sports he was always there. When my dad would punish me he would come in and rescue me and lighten the punishment.

We called him Big-daddy because he told my father what to do. When he moved in with us he saw the other side of me. He saw my father and I arguing and fighting, he saw the monster that I turned into. I even stole and lied to him while he was with us.

But this made no sense. The bridge was in perfect shape. I took Leon card out and slid it into the slot to summons Leon. Within minutes Leon showed up.

Leon said this was a very delicate part of my journey. Many people never get closure concerning those that have passed away. Some find freedom from addiction but there is emptiness deep inside.

I then ask Leon "why was my grandfathers bridge undamaged, and what was I suppose to do?" Leon said "To get closure you must write as you did for everyone else you harmed. Many people go to the burial site and leave letters. For those that can't get to the burial site for whatever reason they find a sacred, peaceful place where they can make their amends, talk to their love ones and ask for forgiveness.

Leon shared with me that his mother and father pass while he was locked up in jail. When it was time to make amends he wrote a letter to both of them. Put each letter in a sealed bottle and tossed it into the ocean.

I then said, "But why was Big-daddy's bridge not on fire like the rest?" Leon said, "Your grandfather is in heaven and he is alright. He knows the path you are taking. This exercise listing all the people you have harmed is not for them, this exercise is for you!" Leon turned and walked away.

I grab the key board and like all the others began to write. When I finished I felt 10 pounds lighter.

There were no bridges left. Like a wounded duck, I made my way over to the elevator, wondering what could possibly be in store next. As the doors opened, Leon stepped out and told me to follow him. He took me to another entrance that led me back to the third floor. He knew exactly what I needed and when I needed it. My own personal angel was looking out for me knowing I was having a hard time putting one foot in front of the other at this point. He sat me down in the grass next to a stream where the sign read, "O Taste and See That the Lord is Good."

After taking a drink from the stream, once again I felt everything was going to be all right. Then he brought me a platter full of fruit. The first piece was from a bush called Security. Then I grabbed the fruit from the tree of Peace. After taking a bite, I stopped beating myself up for what happened in the past. Leon began to read, from a passage in the Bible out of the book of Corinthians chapter 5, verse 17 where it reads, *"Therefore if anyone is in Christ, he is a new creature, old things are passed away; behold, all thing are become new."* The words from the Bible sound like sweet music to my soul. Then I took a bite of the fruit from the tree of Love. Leon said "Learning to love myself is the key to loving others. Even if those loved ones and friends decide not to love you back, you still must love them.

I was in no hurry to go to the next floor, so I just lay back in the grass enjoying God's beauty. Leon told me that because I was now a child of God that I should take on the characteristics of our Father. This is why we return back to the third floor daily so that these characteristics will become ingrained in our spirits and slowly these things will be seen by others.

Far off in the distance, I could see it happening again. The fog that filled my spirit early in this process began to creep over the valley again consuming everything in its path. This time, I got on my knees and I began to thank God as it consumed my whole body. Once again, my spirit jumped as this spirit-filled fog connected with my spirit. This time, I ran and jumped for joy. I leaped through the bushes and across the stream thanking and praising God for reviving me again. After the fog lifted and like a kid in a candy store, combined with a soldier with marching orders in hand, I was ready to continue on to the next floor.

Leon told me before I returned that I should take a walk to one more tree. He led me to the tree of forgiveness, where I grabbed the fruit off of the tree and took a bite. Thunder rang out again in the valley. Once again, a cloud started to form in the sky and it began to move towards us. Knowing what was going to happen next, I closed my eyes as the cloud emptied its damp contents on to the both of us. The sun came out and filled the valley and within seconds we were both completely dry.

Leon then told me to remember God's Word because Satan's job was to remind me of how bad I used to be. He then told me that one definition of forgiveness is *"acting as if it never happened"*.

Leon led me back to the elevator. I pushed the button summoning its arrival and turned and shook Leon's hand. "Just a little touch from God, that's all it takes" Leon shared with a caring smile. I thanked him for being there for me as the doors opened and I got on the elevator.

I Apologize .... Again!

Ninth Floor

Wow! I'm feeling real good right now. "Higher" I thought as the elevator went through the clouds. I was so high in my spirit that I could not fathom going any higher. Again, I said, "Higher." When I looked out of the glass elevator, I saw that I was so high I couldn't see the ground. In the distance, I could see a few elevators still going up and a few descending. Once again, I thought about Carmen. I wondered if she started over or left the building all together. I could only pray for her and today I believe prayer works.

This good feeling I was experiencing was soon about to change. As the doors opened and I walked out of the elevator, it looked like I was back on the eight floor. Down in the valley, I could see fires still burning and smoke filled the air. I looked back inside the elevator making sure I had gotten off on the right floor. There was no mistake. I was on the ninth floor. I decided to follow the trail down to the valley floor. This led me through the jungle and to an opening. Right before I made it to the opening, Leon appeared. He told me that I did not have to do this by myself. As I went through the opening, I looked at him and said, "Do what?" When I looked up, there at the edge of the water sitting at a desk, was my dad. To my surprise, I was on the other side of the lake. My father's head was buried in the screen and he never noticed that we were standing behind him. I asked Leon what was he doing. He told me he was reading what I had sent to him on the computer screen again. I stood there unable to move I hadn't talked to my father in years, wondering how he would react when he saw me. I whispered to Leon, "The last time we were together, it turned into a shouting match." My heart was beating a mile a minute as I tried to put one foot in front of the other.

I looked back at Leon who stood at the edge of the trail. I was standing right behind my dad as he continued to read, and, finally, he felt our presence. He turned around and with a smile on his face, (good sign) he then stood up paused and open his arms wide to receive me, like a little kid I think I fell into his arms. My body went limp in his arms as tears uncontrollably rolled down my cheeks.

With his arms still around me, he whispered in my ear, "All is forgiven son". He called me son I hadn't heard that in years. God is giving me another chance to get it right," I thought to myself. When we finally let each other go, we both had tears running down both of our cheeks. He said, "I'm just happy I got my son back".

As we walked toward the edge of the water, he began to apologize for things he thought he had done. I tried to stop him, but he wanted to continue speaking his mind. He told me he was sorry for not trusting me and for being so hard on me. We both vowed to spend more time with each other and learn how to listen to one another more.

As we walked along the edge of the lake, we both noticed that the fire on the bridge my father sat in front of was extinguished. Leon joined us and I introduced him to my father. Leon said "There was only one way this bridge could be rebuilt and that's one day at a time. This will take a lot of honesty and commitment on both your parts to make this relationship healthy."

He turned to me and said, "We have plenty of time to mend our relationship, but right now you have a bigger hurdle to deal with, which is your mother". I asked him how should I approach her and he said, "It's not as hard as you think, she's just like me, she just wants her son back."

I looked over toward my mother's bridge. I could barely see her because the smoke was so thick. Her bridge was still in flames as I gazed over the lake. I began to pray as I walked toward her. The closer I got to my mother, the faster my heart started beating.

She turned and saw me coming towards her and she got up from the desk put her head in her hands and began to weep. In the background, you could see the bridge burning out of control. When I finally reached her, she looked up and put her arms around me she looked me right in my eyes and told me that she loved me so much.

As she spoke, I said nothing because there was nothing I could say. I could see the strain in her face from the years of worry, staying up all night, crying and praying, scared to answer late night phone calls because she thought it might be the police or morgue. The years of stress was all over her face and had taken a toll on her. She then said "sometimes I would pray the police would pick you up then at least we would know where you were." I hurt the most precious woman in the world and saying, "I'm sorry", or "I won't smoke or drink anymore" was simply not enough. She heard it too many times. I know that the only thing that would fix my mother's pain was for me to be completely free from drugs and alcohol forever.

When she finished talking, she grabbed my hands and immediately started praying. I closed my eyes and agreed with every word that was uttered. When I opened my eyes, I could see peace was resting all over her face, this was a sight that I had not seen in a long time. I gave her a hug and told her I loved her and thanked her for always praying for me. I told her "If it were not for your prayers, I would probably still be drinking and using or, even worse, dead in my grave."

She hugged me again. As I held her, I could see the fire on the bridge slowly extinguishing itself. We talked a little while longer, and I told her that I still had work to do. In order for me to walk away from my past totally free and clean, I have to continue making amends to those people whom I had harmed.

We said our goodbyes, and I proceeded to walk down toward the next bridge. I began thanking and praising the Lord for giving me the opportunity to mend my relationship with my parents. But then it hit me, "What if I don't make it? "What if I let my mother down again?" I quickly stop that thought and cast it down in the name of Jesus. It was then that I noticed how quickly the enemy attacked my mind just after God had blessed me. I knew I had to continue on. There were many more people I had to make amends to.

The next bridge if we were staying in the order of the 8th floor was Gail my ex-fiancée. Her bridge looked like a burning inferno and most of the bridge had fallen into the lake. I stood there and looked at it knowing it would take the mighty power of God and an act of congress for her to listen to anything I had to say. Before I continued on, I decided I was in no hurry, so I went to the room called "CHANGE".

As I was walking into the room called "CHANGE," I ran into Annette, who was just leaving the meeting. It was so good to see someone out of the faithful 12. I asked her had she seen anyone else from our group. She told me that she seen Hazel, Wendell, and Keith, on some of the previous floors. They were all doing as well as expected. Going through this process called recovery is not easy, but we take the process one step, one day at a time. She gave me a big hug and told me that she was headed back to the 7th floor.

I made it to the room just before the speaker went up to the podium. To my surprise, it was Leon my sponsor. Leon started off by sharing how he spent most of his young adult life in and out of juvenile hall and working fire camps. He talked about being a part of gangs and living a criminal lifestyle. I was shocked, because you could never look at him today and tell he at one time lived that way. This new life of recovery was certainly good to him, and I wanted what he had. After sharing briefly about his past, he began talking about living free and a life in recovery.

Leon said "everything you learn in this building if applied will help you make it through life, but making it through this building will take a lot of patience and a lot of courage. I know you are getting a lot of information and it can be overwhelming, but it will be enforced as you continue to come back to these meetings".

Take your time, you can only work on what God puts before you one-day-at-a-time. One-day-at-a-time, we make amends; one-day-at-a-time, we practice powerlessness; one-day-at-a-time, we trust God; and one-day-at-a-time, we don't drink and use. One-day-at-a-time is one of the most powerful tools used by people who go through this building. One-day-at-a-time makes any task reachable. *I will not drink or use today*, I will not allow my character defects to run my life today. Just for today, I will be the best person I can be. We have to let people be who they are, and if God changes them, so be it. Acceptance is key and we cannot change people, places, or things.

On the day you get it in your spirit that you cannot change people, places or things the process of recovery get's easier. Each challenge put before us is a great opportunity for us to trust God and sometimes change. Those who are afraid to trust God miss the great things that God has in store for them.

God allows us to go through many test or a trial because each challenge, situation, or circumstance proves to be an opportunity to grow. The key to a better life is learning how to trust God in everything you do."

It was time to move on. It was time to face the rest of my loved ones and friends. When I arrived back onto the ninth floor, I could see Gail's bridge still engulfed in flames. Through the smoke, I could see she had not moved from the desk as she was reading the letter I sent to her. It was as if she were reading it over and over again. She finally noticed me from about 15 feet away. Tears were pouring down her cheeks as she stood up. All I could do is remain quiet and continue walking towards her.

She broke the silence and asked, "How could you been so mean to me!" Why, why, why, what did I ever do to you but love you, as she cried uncontrollably." Saying nothing, she continued talking, "When you said you loved me, were you lying?" By this time, tears were running down my face.

I wanted to tell her what I had learned, here, in this building and that my addiction is truly classified as a disease and a sickness but at this point, that would have been a waste of time. She really didn't want an answer from me. There were so many things she had to get off her chest.

"I hate that you came into my life acting like you cared." While she was pouring out her heart, I just silently talk to God and asked him to, once again, please forgive me for breaking Gail's heart.

After every outburst she belted out, I felt more and more helpless than the time before, so much so that I just grabbed her and held her close to me. Gail began beating me in the chest sobbing uncontrollably. She finally calmed down with her head buried in my chest. I just held her close for what seemed like eternality. All I could say was, "I'm sorry" over and over and over again.

There was a area near the lake set up for times such as this where we could sit down and talk. I sat there in silence, as she sobbed with her head buried in her hands. I had never felt so helpless in all of my life. Finally, Gail told me that she had never loved anyone before me, and her life was scarred because of me.

She said she read the letter and she believed I was sincere, but she would be a fool to ever trust me or anyone ever again. All she wanted to do was get on with her life.

I told her I understood and would not bother her ever again. I left, and returned to the third floor. I sat down amongst the flowers asking God to forgive me again. Here I was in this building getting my life together, but what I had done in my past had ruined other peoples' lives. I sat there for hours praying for Gail and all the people I harmed.

I returned to the ninth floor to find the fires on the remaining bridges were not as intense as Gail's bridge. Most of my friends and relatives just wanted me to get my life together and be the person they once knew before I started drinking and using.

I now understood the pain and suffering that my loved ones went through. I found out how much they loved me, and for that, I would be forever grateful.

I finally put a period behind most of the people I used and abused, and it was time to leave this floor. After spending some time with Leon, I returned to the glass elevator that would take me to, yet, another experience. Slowly the doors closed behind me. It took me up through more clouds. The sun was shining brightly. There were elevators going up through the clouds as far as the eye could see.

As the elevator began to stop, a sign appeared on a message board. It read "Welcome to the 10th floor. You have almost completed your journey, but it is far from being over."

10th Step

Are You Willing To Take The Test?

A-B-C-D or Fail?

Tenth Floor

When I walked out of the elevator, Leon met me. With a big smile on his face he said "It's ok to take your time, Rome wasn't built in a day. Don't worry your doing fine", there was something about being on the right track that made me feel good about myself. I had to be doing something right because I only thought about drinking or using once maybe twice during this entire time in this building and that was a miracle in itself.

Throughout my entire life, I had never completed anything that I started. Everyone around me consider me to be a failure. People always told me that I would never amount to anything and, after a while, I started to believe what was being said. Leon reminded me that the journey was not over and, for the rest of my life; I would have to apply these principles to my life.

For the rest of my life, living right and striving to be good in the sight of God will be my primary goal. Leon talked about the perfect walk of Christ and how, we, as Christians would forever strive to be like Christ. The Bible describes this process like this: we are always *"Pressing towards the mark of the high calling in Christ Jesus."* Trudging through life's challenges, trials, fears, and disappointments is a continuous process. What we do is learn how to put one foot in front of the other constantly trusting in God along the way.

Leon led me to a small room. Inside this room was a table with one t-shirt on it. I picked up the shirt and on the front of the shirt the writing said, "Can You Pass The Test?" As soon as I put the T-shirt on, the lights went off and it was so dark that I couldn't see one foot in front of me. A cool breeze flowed through the room and throughout my entire body. I could not put my finger on it, but something had changed. Finally, the lights came back on. I asked Leon what was going on. He smiled and said, "You will soon see."

We walked toward the door that was on the other side of the room. When I opened the door, I was surprised to see Leon following me. On previous floors, this is where He, disappeared. When the door closed behind us, the lights came on and we were standing in my apartment again. I looked at Leon, and he told me to just wait a few moments.

Suddenly, the bedroom door opened, and through the door, in walked a replica of myself. I was, literally, walking towards me. Woe! Or a person who looked just like me, walked right by us and he didn't see us standing there. Leon then said, "He can't see us, we are invisible to him, but that is you." Your job on this floor is to follow your replica around and give yourself a grade as you go through different situations or tests. The grades are: A, B, C, D, or F. An "A" is for outstanding (you handled the situation in a Godly manner.). "B" is very good (you handled the situation well, but the overall situation could have been handled better.) "C" for satisfactory, (your situation needs work, you must do better.). "D" stands for disappointing (You have to do better). Finally, "F" stands for Fail (You didn't try.).

"I will meet with you daily to go over some of the things that went on in that day. Your job is to explain how you viewed yourself in every circumstance, situation, or test." He gave me a pin and notepad and left the room.

When I turned back to observe myself (my replica), I was sitting on the couch reading the paper with the TV on. So far, this was perfectly harmless and I didn't have very much to write about. It was now approaching 8:00 am and Frank whom I shall refer to as Frank (#2), and myself, Frank #1. Frank (#2) got up from the couch, grabbed his keys, and made his way out the door. He got into his car and started it up, and I climbed into the back seat.

We made our way down the street when suddenly a car came out of nowhere, literally, running the stop sign nearly colliding with us. If Frank (#2) did not have such quick reflexes, the car would have hit us. Once everything settled, the person in the other car began to blow his horn at us as if we were in the wrong. Frank (#2) blew back at him, and they both exchanged some very heated words before Frank (#2) made a right turn and continued on.

This was the perfect time to examine "Frank's (#2) reaction to the car incident. I had to agree with Frank (#2). This incident was certainly not his fault, but how Frank (#2) reacted to the situation was what I had to grade: A, B, C, D, or F; what did he deserve? I gave him a "C", because he was powerless over the guy blowing his horn; however, Frank's (#2) reaction could have been better. There was a time in my life when that was the perfect opportunity to lose my temper.

After that encounter, Frank (#2) continued on to a computer store to pick up some parts. Frank (#2) was anticipating a call from a guy name John he recently met at a dinner party. He needed some work done on his computer at his home. John also had a very attractive sister that he introduced to Frank (#2).

John owned a nice house on the west side of town. He had just built an office in his home and was having problems with his computer. Frank (#2) agreed to fix John's computer and also add more memory to the hard drive so that the computer would operate at a faster pace. Any other time, Frank (#2) would have charged $400 dollars for such a job, but Frank (#2) was really attracted to John's sister and John knew this. Frank (#2) thought this would be the perfect opportunity to score some valuable points with John and meet John's sister.

While in the store, Frank (#2) received a call from John informing him that his sister would be dropping by and would he like to come over. He also suggested Frank (#2) bring his tools to fix the computer. Because John was willing to put in a good word to his sister, Frank (#2) agreed to fix the computer for half price. After fixing and adding memory to the computer, John's sister finally showed up. To Frank's (#2) and my surprise, John's sister was with her fiancé. Frank (#2) was shocked and upset to find out she was engaged to be married! Once it was clear that John had used him, Frank (#2) never let John know how he felt. To the contrary, the sly grin on John's face let Frank

(#2) know that he had just gotten played. Frank knew that John had taken advantage of him by using his sister to get a cheaper price to work on the computer. Frank (#2) received his $200 dollars and left the house without saying a word. Deep down inside, however, Frank knew he had played the game and loss.

The whole time this was going on I, Frank (#1) took notes and figured so far that this was easy to examine. I gave Frank (#2) a "B" for keeping his cool and not saying anything about being deceived by John.

After leaving John's house, we both got in the car and left. While driving home, Frank (#2) was still pretty upset and he was uncomfortable having been used.

After getting a bite to eat, Frank (#2) calmed down by turning on the TV and going to sleep in his favorite chair. I, Frank (#1) decided to go to the room called "CHANGE". It was time to check in. First I had to go to the room where I first became invisible so that I could become visible again.

When I arrived at the room called "CHANGE", to my surprise, there sitting in the back of the room was Ronnie the sales man the brother that wouldn't walk through the door on the first floor in the room called "Willingness". Praise the Lord! Big Ronnie never gave up. I tapped him on the shoulder and his eyes lit up when he saw me. He stood up and gave me a big bear hug.

Ronnie then turned and introduced me to his Sponsor, Lucky. Lucky was a tall muscular guy with wire rim glasses on. We shook hand and ask me what floor was I on? I told him "floor #10" and he smiled. He then said "examining yourself is a lifelong process.

"Never arriving is the key". Lucky then quoted a scripture *"no man is perfect no not one, and we all fall short to the glory of God.*

We sat down, and Ronnie told me how glad he was to see me and how it took him three months and a little help from his parole officer to continue on in recovery. He told me he was headed to the 4th floor and he just accepted Christ into his life. We gave each other a high-five and as we grinned uncontrollably; it was virtually impossible to peel the smiles off of both of our faces.

Ronnie wanted to share with me why he hesitated when he was on the second floor. I abruptly stopped him in his tracks, and told him that wasn't important, and that I was glad he was here. He gave me another hug, and we gave our attention to the meeting that was just beginning to take place.

A middle-aged woman made her way to the podium and introduced herself as Amahri. She shared that she was married with four kids and was a closet drinker. She talked about facing our fears, humble ourselves, and getting out the way so that God can change our lives.

She said that her problems began 29 years ago growing up in a dysfunctional family. Her mother and father were well-off and spent a lot of time traveling around the country, thus leaving her and her older brother to raise themselves. Amahri shared that she started drinking at 13 years old but it progressively got worse about 14 years ago after her husband left her for a younger woman. Within two and a half years, she had become a full-blown alcoholic. This was her third time going through *Recovery Tower* and, as of this date, she had 6 years clean and sober.

The first time she came through *Recovery Tower*, she did not think she was as bad as all the stories she heard in and out of the rooms of recovery, and as a result, she didn't take recovery seriously. The second time she got well quick. She left after four months. Not a month went by before she was drinking again, and this time it got even worse. This time around, she experienced blackouts; rape and she even got pulled over for drunk driving and spent a weekend in jail. Ronnie leaned over toward me and told me that he was headed back to the third floor. We shook hands and he and his sponsor Lucky departed.

Next, Amahri began to talk about her tenth floor experience. She said, "The key to passing each test on this floor is to examine every action and every reaction honestly. The most important part of examining yourself is understanding your motives behind each action. Many of you thought the drugs and alcohol was the problem but here on this floor you will be faced with the real you and what makes you tick.

Amahri then ask a question "if you still have an urge to drink and use raise your hands". Everyone looked around at each other and out of 25 people in the room only 6 raised their hand. I was not sure about how long other people had been in this building, but I had been in *Recovery Tower* for 10 months and the last time I thought about drinking and using was when I was on the second floor or somewhere thereabout.

She then thanked those individuals who raised their hands for being honest and said "drugs and alcohol is only 5% of your problem, 95% of the problem is you. On this floor you will be introduce to the real you daily! Then you take that person and line him up with God and you'll see how far you have to go."

"We, in *Recovery Tower*, came into this building and our top priority was to stay free from drugs and alcohol. In our quest to stay free, we found out we had a lot more problems.

Living the way God would have us to live takes precedence over everything else. God is at the top – He's Number #1. By doing this, God would eliminate, remove, or heal us from the drug and alcohol problem or problems we face.

When I walked out of the meeting, Leon was standing there waiting for me. He asked me how my first day went on the tenth floor as I examined myself. I first started off with the car incident. After explaining what happened, I told him that the person who almost caused the accident was certainly not Frank's (#2) fault; however, getting into a verbal confrontation and reacting the way he did was clearly wrong, so I gave him a "C". The right thing to do was to ignore this person and move on.

Leon looked at me and said, "Is that it?", as if I had left something out. I paused for a minute, thought about it again, and said, "Yes". He told me to take a seat. I detected a little disgust in his voice. He said, "First, his problems didn't start with the car incident; his problems started by leaving the house without having prayed. Next, he should have thanked God for the quick reflexes and for His divine protection. Of course, Frank (#2) was wrong for losing his temper, but he never asked God for forgiveness after the verbal altercation ended.

Forgiveness puts us back in right standing with God after we have fallen short. Forgiveness helps us to humble ourselves, realizing we have to take a look at our anger issues. In examining ourselves, it keeps the character defects, in this case, "anger", ever before us. The Bible says, *Be angry, but sin not.*

After sitting there and listening, I clearly dropped the ball on that one. He must have sensed that I was upset with myself and said, "Our goal is to seek progress rather than perfection, and it gets better as we grow. So don't worry about it."

I looked down at my note pad and the next set of examination notes. "How incomplete are these notes I thought?" I guess Leon sensed my questioning the notes and told me not to worry about it. He said, "As you practice examining yourself daily, you will get better at seeing all your faults, and shortcomings. This is one reason you have a sponsor, someone that understands this process called recovery and will not co-sign your character defects." Then he asked me if I saw anything else on this first day of examining myself?

The next incident I really didn't think was worth mentioning, but it was more of a victory for Frank (#2), so I wrote it down anyway. I shared how Frank (#2) held his peace after fixing the computer for half the price and not saying anything at all about being deceived by John. "Frank (#2)" did very well, and I gave him a "B".

Once again, Leon said, "Is that it?" This time with a smile on his face, he said, "You have to learn how to take a better look at yourself, your actions, and also your motives behind what you do and say. " A good way to examine yourself is to examine the motive? If you understand this part of the process, you will grow by leaps and bounds."

I sat there trying to figure out what I did wrong. He told me what I'd missed in this examination was your motives. He was clearly wrong in the beginning. Just because it did not turn out the way he wanted, he still did not have a right to get angry.

You wasn't giving John a reduced price because he was a friend; you was doing the job just to get closer to John's sister. So, your motives were wrong from the start. Since the outcome was not what you had planned, you had no right to get upset.

People who play games with other people's lives have to suffer the consequences when the game does not rule in their favor. If you had remained professional throughout the ordeal, you never would have lost the $200 dollars in the first place. He also told me that my prayer life leaves lot to be desired. There is no doubt that you love God, but his trust level is very low."

As Leon was talking, it hit me like a ton of bricks that he was talking about me! My motives were wrong, and my prayer life leaves a lot to be desired, and I lacked trust in God.

As he spoke, I did not hear a word he said as I could only think about my relationship with God. He was right. I do love God, but something was missing. Was it this trust issue he spoke about? Finally, I redirected my focus back on what he was saying. I interrupted him in the middle of his speech. I told him that he was right; I still put more trust in myself than in God. "But, why" I asked myself? Why was it so hard to go to God with everything? After all, God has done for me what I could not or cannot do for myself, and I am still trying to be in charge.

Is it this whole thing about humility all over again, or do I simply have a problem with authority?" Leon looked at me and said, "This is a new life for you, why do you still trust solely in you?" After thinking about it for a minute, I told him that maybe I still thought I had some power or maybe I believe God is too busy for some of these trivial matters.

Leon pulled out his Bible and began to read *"Trust in the Lord with all thine heart and lean not unto thine own understanding and in all thy ways acknowledge Him and He will direct your path."* This scripture tells us that as Christians, we are to acknowledge God and ask for his direction in everything we do. Not going to God for everything shows immaturity, or your lack of trust in Him.

Be careful you don't push God out of your life, once again, leaning on our own understanding. God has ordered our steps, but He will not make us walk in them. If we surrender to His Word and to His spirit that dwells deep down inside of us, our going and continuing in the right direction becomes easier.

When examining ourselves, we have to ask the question, "What is our motive behind our actions?" "Why am I doing this?" "Is this action to help someone else so that God can get the glory, or is action to satisfy my own wants, desires, or aspirations? Whether the action is good or bad, we have to examine ourselves.

Next, we have to ask the question, "What role did we have to play in the situation? "What did you do that was instrumental in the situation taking a turn for the worse?" What part did you play in the situation going bad?" Those who ask themselves this question grow by leaps and bounds and are able to prepare themselves for being more successful in relationships and possibly prevent more of these failures from occurring in the future.

Leon asked me if I was ready to go back to the tenth floor. Without hesitating, I told him "yes." I was determined to get this part of my life right. To abandon ship now, or run from this challenge, would be foolish and doing this would not help me to obtain this better life that I earnestly long for.

He took me back to the room where I had to go through that process of disappearing all over again. Before I went in, he told me to be watchful and alert. The enemy is like a roaring lion seeking who he might devour. I walked through the room and once my disappearing act had come to an end, I found myself at a little league baseball game. As I looked around, I finally spotted Frank (#2) sitting in the stands watching my nephew play baseball. Our family is very close and we loved spending time with each other. I really use to enjoy this recreational activity that is when I was not drinking or using. There were many people in the stands watching the game and rooting for both sides.

As the game went on and the excitement began to build, the game changed drastically when a close call was called at the plate by the umpire. The kid that was on my nephew's team was called safe at the plate. Half of the people in the stands went crazy believing the call by the umpire was a proper call. Of course, the other half of the spectators appeared to be thoroughly convinced the umpire made the wrong call.

One fan who was sitting one row in front of Frank (#2) really lost his temper, and he began yelling at the umpire and then switched to the people in the stands who were supporting my nephew's team. Knowing Frank as I did, (and I know him well) I knew it is only so much he would take. The guy kept yelling at everyone and finally Frank (#2) told him to sit down and shut up. The guy turned around and saw that Frank (#2) was two feet taller and 60 pounds heavier. It was evident that the guy did not want any problem with Frank (#2) was until he turned around. After seizing up the situation, the guy sat down and was quite as a church house mouse. The game ended, and my nephew's team won by one controversial run.

Leon appeared and asked the question, "What grade did you give yourself?" I told him I gave him (remembering Leon's earlier advise), a "D". "Why?" he inquired. I told him for two reasons: 1) Frank (#2) did not pray about the situation before he acted. A quick prayer asking God to keep him calm would have worked. In addition, Frank (#2) did not practice being powerless over this person. Who put Frank (#2) in charge of fixing this person? Frank should have kept his peace instead of telling the guy to sit down and shut up.

Leon said "A very good observation, but what would have happened if the guy would have been just as big as you, or not afraid to stand up to you? This was a perfect time to practice powerless. How many kids would have witnessed two men fighting over a baseball game? What type of message would that have sent? Living righteous and holy and being prayerful will keep you humble and in perfect peace with God."

Then he asked me if I would like to continue moving forward, and I responded, "yes".

He told me the key to change is living what you leaned in recovery and to learn from your previous mistakes. He turned and took me to another door, and before I walked through that door, he told me that I could find Frank (#2) across town on 42nd street, and I would have to catch a cab to start my examination.

As I walked through the door, I found myself on a busy street where everybody seemed to be in a hurry. I walked to the edge of the street and tried to hail a cab. After about fifteen minutes on the street, finally a cab pulled over. As I walked up to the car, a man almost knocked me down as he jumped hurriedly into the cab that I had flagged down. I was furious. He looked at me, smiled, and locked the doors. I gave him a gesture that was not too godly as the cab pulled off and simultaneously it hit me like a lightning bolt. I was not invisible anymore, and I had just failed, yet, another test. When I looked around, I saw Leon walking toward me. I could not look him in the eye, I failed the test. (I should have known something was going on when the cab driver saw me and pulled over because I was supposed to be invisible).

Dumbfounded Leon led me to a small coffee shop on the street. I couldn't believe I had blown that situation so quickly, and just that fast, the test was over. I guess there was nothing really happening on 42nd Street. What made it so bad was I really thought I was better than what my actions displayed. With my head down, I apologized for my actions and for failing the test. Leon told me that I did not have to apologize to him, but insisted that I should ask God for forgiveness and continue moving forward. Knowing what to do after taking a test is just as important as taking the test. He also said that people in recovery have to understand that a test can occur at any time, and these tests are designed to make us better if we would only recognize we are being tested.

A failed test can turn out to be a blessing in disguise if we learn from our failures. He continued on by saying sometimes God will allow Satan to tempt you and detour you from the blessings that God has for you. Even though the devil's job is to kill, steal, and destroy, he is not able to do any more than God will allow him to do. As recovering people, we have to always be on guard and be ever so mindful that a test can present itself at any time.

Once again, he asked me if I was ready to continue on this tenth floor journey. I told him that I was in no hurry and indicated that I would rather go to the room called "CHANGE".

Through another door, I found myself in the room called "CHANGE". I started looking for a friendly face, someone whom I could talk too about these back to back failures I had just experienced. I had grown close to Leon since entering *Recovery Tower*, but I needed someone who was going through this building as a client. In no time, it hit me again, "Pray before I go." (Was this another test? Is everything a test?) I began to pray and asked God to help me make it through this tenth floor and to help me change. Before I could get the prayer out of my mouth, someone tapped me on my shoulders. When I looked around, it was Shorty. "Wow!" I thought to myself. God wasted no time in answering this prayer. I have got to take this prayer thing more seriously. We embraced, and I began to tell him about how I had failed on the tenth floor and nearly every test. After about three minutes of "crying the blues" and telling Shorty how completing this life - changing recovery course was beginning to feel like an impossible task. Shorty simply looked at me and said, "Quit crying, welcome to your new life". Once again Shorty showed no compassion, no sympathy at all. He quickly apologized and told me he still has some areas he's working on.

At the same time, however, the words he spoke were from his heart and he meant what he said. Crying the blues helps nothing. Shorty then said, "Nobody is perfect - no not one; we either get better or stay the same because there was no in between.

At this point we have to begin looking at recovery as a blessing. Not many people get a chance to change the course of their lives using a structured method that works.

This is why I liked Shorty in the first place. He honest and keeps it real. Shorty was right; coming into recovery has been one of the best things that ever happen to me. I knew I could not go back to my old life. I had to continue on in the recover process in order to get better, and stop crying the blues.

I finally located Leon and, this time, I asked him if he thought I was ready to move on to the next floor. To my surprise, he responded by saying, "Yes" Examining yourself is something you will do for the rest of your life. The key to the tenth floor is to be willing to take an honest look at yourself and make the necessary changes.

He led me to the elevator, and I stepped on. Once again, I looked out into this world of elevators and blue skies. What a ride I thought. One day at a time I will be the best person that I can be. The elevator stopped, and before the doors opened, I said a quick prayer, and then prepared myself for what was next.

Don't Get Amnesia

Check your oil, water, and transmission fluid daily,
you'll get better use out of your vehicle.

Eleventh Floor

Once the elevator doors opened onto the eleventh floor, the room directly in front of me looked familiar. I stepped out onto a platform similar to the one on the second floor. In front of me were railroad tracks. I looked to the right of me and through the fog appeared another transparent monorail. This one had two seats, whereas the other had more. Riding inside this monorail was Leon. The glass doors opened, and I stepped inside, and Leon greeted me with a warm, godly hug.

We strapped ourselves as the monorail moved slowly into a cloudbank, where it picked up speed. We rode for a few minutes and we stopped suddenly above a room that looked very familiar; we were on the first floor. The monorail came to a complete stop and, from where we were sitting; I could see the "Powerless", "Willingness", "Honesty", and "Acceptance" rooms below us. In each room, there were people going through the process of recovery. It seemed like only yesterday when I started going through this part of the process. I thought about how many times I wanted to leave, because it was in these rooms I had to totally surrender.

Leon asked me, "What did you remember most about these rooms?" I told him that the Honesty/Acceptance room was brutal because not only did I have to face who I really was, but I realized that I did not like what I saw in me. My whole life was a lie, and I struggle with who I was. I prayed to God that I never put myself in that position again.

The "Willingness" room was where I was given a chance to surrender, and the knowledge I received changed my thinking. This is the place where we lost some of our friends because they were not willing to trust in this process and go forward. The concept of faith made a lot of since to me in this room, and I learned you have to step out and believe. Faith was something that I could not see with my physical eyes, but I had to trust and believed.

The "Powerless" room turned out to be one of the most powerful tools in this recovery walk. Still today, I'm still working on "Powerlessness", but I understand the concept, and thank God for it. There is power in being powerless. What a theory. I have to always be mindful that the power that I have is on loan to me from God. When problems arise I have to tap into God's power for the solution.

Today, I have a better chance of succeeding if I can remember this "Powerless" concept. The quicker I become powerless the faster God's powerful will rule my life. Powerless is also great when dealing with my controlling issues. I have no power over people, places and things.

The monorail started up again and slowly began to move away from the first floor. As I looked down through the glass monorail and saw people stuck at the door of "Willingness." I said a quick prayer for them, and we moved on. We rode for a few minutes and shortly thereafter arrived at the second floor.

It was on the second floor where I was introduced to prayer and the importance of studying the Word of God. It was on this floor where I learned God had been with me all my life even when I didn't know Him.

There was a group of people entering the room filled with books. I could see another group arriving at the end where they picked up their Bible. Once again, something leaped inside me as one young lady grabbed her Bible. As I looked closer, I saw it was Carmen. She came back. Tears of joy ran down my face as she surrendered to this process one more time. All I could do was thank and praise God for being a God of another chance.

The monorail slowly inched its way forward, slowed up, and stopped over the booth where I prayed for the first time. I guess for people that have a relationship with God this means nothing, but for me this will be a day I will never forget.

The next floor was the third floor, and I could see the beautiful staircase that led to the large doors. There was no way I was going to pass this opportunity up and not stop and visit this floor. This is where I accepted Jesus Christ into my life and surrendered to this new life. This is where I decided to become a 24/7 Christian.

On the other side of the big doors was the 3rd floor paradise. As far as the eyes could see were the beautiful trees and flowers. I looked and Leon and he said "Do you want to visit this floor?" I said "Sure" At that moment the monorail stopped and a tube appeared which transported us down to the third floor.

As we were going down, I could see, off in the distance, the thick fog moving toward us. Joy filled my body as I anticipated what was going to happen next. As soon as we touched the ground, I took off running towards the fog that was coming toward us. When I entered the fog, it consumed my body and I allowed the fog to fill me again. From my head to my toe, I felt the presence of God consume me. "Fill me again," I whispered, fill me again!"

As the fog lifted, we ate from every fruit that was on this floor. Then we drank from the stream that gave life. Once again, I was standing next to the sign that said, "O taste and see that the Lord is Good," and I yelled at the top of my lungs, "Oh, yes, He is!" We both stayed on this third floor another day, then returned to the monorail.

Next, the monorail appeared over the room called "CHANGE" where Leon said "your victories will be won in rooms just like this as long as you stay honest". Leon suggested that after leaving *Recovery Tower* I go to these meeting room call "Change" every day for 90 days straight. This would set a solid foundation for the rest of my life.

For days the monorail revisited each floor. It was amazing how much I had grown and how much I learned in such a short amount of time.

After going through every floor, we returned to the platform on the eleventh floor where Leon said never forget what you've learned in this building and apply it to your life.

We both got off the monorail and made our way to the elevator which now has been very instrumental in my life.

Before we moved to the twelfth floor, I decided to go to the room called "CHANGE". As I walked up to the meeting place, I saw some familiar faces standing outside. These were my friends who started this journey with me. When they saw me, we all ran toward each other and embraced one another. Shorty, Ronnie, Bobby, Nyna, Hazel, Annette, Rodney, Keith, and Wendell and I were all together again. Everybody had a personal story to tell about this building called *Recovery Tower*.

We talked about the process of recovery and how it had changed our lives. We talked about how much we loved God and how we had been rescued and given another chance at life. Once again, Shorty shared something that spoke volumes. He said that God was not only our Father, but now he was Lord over our lives which means however He wants to guide us he can. We all agreed we'd serve God for the rest of our lives.

After spending what seemed like hours talking about our journey in *Recovery Tower*, we knew that we could go on and on and on, but we knew we had to go our separate ways. We exchanged phone numbers and promised to stay in touch with each other. Before we departed, we all formed a circle and grabbed each other's hands and asked Shorty to lead us in prayer. When he finished, we all headed to our respective floors.

As I made it to my elevator, Leon was there to meet me. The doors opened, and we both entered the elevator. I was a little nervous knowing that I was headed to the last floor.

Somebody Told You

You Can't Keep This Freedom Unless You Give It Away

Twelfth Floor

After the door closed, Leon pushed the button to the twelfth floor. Slowly, the elevator began to move. As we looked out the elevator overlooking this magnificent building, Leon began to remind me that it was God who put the *process of recovery* together for addicts, alcoholics, overeaters, workaholics, codependents, gamblers and anyone who was addicted to anything or anybody. As I looked through the glass at God's glory, I could not peal the smile off my face.

As the elevator continued to climb, Leon continued to talk about how many people will never know God and experience His goodness and His power because no one shared the Good News to them. He told me that it was my job to carry the message of freedom to the addict-alcoholic who was still suffering and also to anyone who would listen.

Leon talked about the enemy, Satan, who was very upset with me. He hates the fact that you have a relationship with God. Satan job is to discourage your walk with God. He is a liar and the truth is not in him.

One day you will see that drugs and alcohol will not be you main problem but until that day comes it is your #1 concern. Everything you've learned and gained in recovery will be destroyed if you take one hit or drink.

"Satan usually attacks believers in the area of disobedience, and if you don't examine yourself daily, challenge yourself to live better by living the Word of God, continue making meetings your addiction will return. "

The last thing he said before the doors opened was to never arrive. Simply put, no one should ever think that he or she has come to the end of recovery. Those who "arrive" stop working on themselves, and they elevate themselves as if they do not have any work to do on themselves. In this mindset, these individuals are no longer teachable and, therefore, no longer reachable.

When the doors opened onto the twelfth floor, there was something very strange, but familiar about this floor. A dark mist seemed to hover over the room, and the light was very dim.

As I looked around, I could see people with no joy and no hope, and sadness on their faces. On the other side of the room there was an elevator. Above the elevator, was an arrow pointing up. I could see people standing there waiting for the doors to open. Others were sitting in corners drinking coffee and really doing nothing.

"Lord, have mercy; I was back in the basement. " I was back in the very same place where I started over a year ago.

A weird feeling came over me, and I looked to Leon who told me it was my turn to help someone. It was my turn to give back what so freely was given to me.

He told me that in order to keep this peace and freedom I had, I must give everything I learned in *Recovery Tower* away to someone in need of help.

This part of the process is critical; the newcomer is the life blood of *recovery program*. One addict/alcoholic helping another is therapeutic.

It's hard to drink or us when you have your arms around someone telling them how to be free.

He told me to take my pick and pointed to the addicts/alcoholics in the basement waiting to get on the elevator pointing "up". Then he turned around and got back onto the elevators we just exit.

As the elevator doors began to close in front of him, Leon said, "If you ever wonder why your life was spared from a horrible death, or if you ever wonder what your calling is, remember this..." and the doors closed before he could finish. In large white letters on the closed door read "YOU WERE SAVED TO SERVE."

I turned around and noticed a guy sitting in a corner crying his eyes out. I also noticed another guy eating like he hadn't had a meal in weeks.

A scripture came to mind "*The harvest is surely ripe, but the labors are few.*" I knew then that it was time for me to give back!

For more information about:
- Faith-based Recovery
- Speaking engagements

Contact Dr. Ronald Simmons at
- freenone@msn.com
- 323 855-4695

15166372R00126

Made in the USA
San Bernardino, CA
20 September 2014